Common Threads

celebrating Life with Down Syndrome

Cynthia S. Kidder and Brian Skotko
Photography by Kendra Dew

Common Threads

Celebrating Life with Down Syndrome

Library of Congress Card Number 2001117129

Common Threads, Celebrating Life with Down Syndrome: Essays compiled from families blessed with a loved one with Down syndrome.

First Edition

ISBN 1-930868-04-9

Stories compiled/written by Cynthia S. Kidder, Brian Skotko or otherwise noted.

Photography by Kendra Dew, Kendra Dew Photographic, Inc.

Edited by Shelley Ottenbacher

Graphic Design by Lee Ann Gusmano, Adesso Design

Printing by Clark Graphics, Inc.

Bindery by Dekker Bookbinding, Inc.

To receive consideration for future publications, please submit stories to the publisher by mail, fax or email.

Band of Angels Press
3048 Charlwood Drive
Rochester Hills, Michigan 48306
Fax: 01-248-377-0206
www.bandofangels.com

PRINTED IN THE USA

This book is dedicated to
Jordan and Kristin,
for making our lives whole

Gratitudes

Kendra Dew, who since our first project together, has seen the beauty of all children through the lens of her camera. Her warmth with the children is radiated in the studio, on location and in her daily life. Her attention to detail is a great counter-balance to my big-picture style. She has made me appreciate the importance of the fine details.

Lee Ann Gusmano, who took raw text and beautiful photograhy and turned them into the book you now see. She, too, shares the vision of a more understanding and beautiful world. Her delicate style and gentle ways make working together carefree.

Jim Decker at John Christian Bindery, who has provided financial support over the years. Jim and Robert Decker have also directed us to great resources and suppliers.

As a small publishing company, Band of Angels Press needed financial support in order to undertake a project of this magnitude. Over the past years, Clark Graphics of Warren, Michigan, has been a hidden supporter of our work. Expecting no recognition, the people at Clark Graphics have believed in us enough to proceed with printing while providing generous payment terms. At every turn, the principals at Clark Graphics expressed confidence that we would be successful. Thank you Judy Clark, Jeff Clark, Patrick Wagner and all of the printing staff. Without you, truly, there is no way this book would have seen publication.

Acknowledgements

Common Threads is the result of shared dreams and great teamwork. Thank you to all the hundreds of people who submitted stories from which we chose. We read and re-read stories, had conference calls to defend favorites, and ultimately agreed to interview over 50 people for the stories featured in this book. Thank you for trusting us with your personal stories. We also acknowledge:

David Koppenhaver, Ph.D., Gustavus Adolphus College, an expert in disabilities research, for reviewing the content and accuracy of our research summaries.

Allison Skotko, for compiling the data from our surveys.

Carol Waltenbaugh, for administrative support.

Kristin O'Neill, for organizing files, stories and photos to keep us on track!

Kristine Stiles, Ph.D., of the Department of Art at Duke University, for her advice on our research summary "A Madonna in Mantua."

Members of the Arts Theme House at Duke University, for their assistance with the initial mailings for this project.

Brian especially acknowledges:

Gary and Sharon Skotko, for their long-standing support of this project.

Kristin Skotko, for making my life whole.

Cynthia especially acknowledges:

Ray and Ethel Waltenbaugh, for taking care of many of the daily mailing and shipping chores to enable me to spend more time writing and creating.

Sherry Viola, who erased doubts and encouraged me to continue—she helped me believe in the value of this project.

My husband, Bill, and my sons Kevin, Harper and Jordan, who have worked in every capacity imaginable to facilitate making the company strong. When I grew tired of all the hard work and low pay, it was Harper who reminded me it was never about the money. We have a message and want it to be heard.

Finally, to every swim coach, teacher, parent, soccer coach, physician, piano teacher, employer and pastor who saw and explored the potential of someone with Down syndrome, *Thank you*. Without a doubt, there are some amazing people out there, and they are integrated into your world and mine.

Contents

Introduction

As a mother of a child with Down syndrome, I have been astonished at every possible juncture at the discrepancy between the commonly held predictions for my son and his actual accomplishments. I firmly believe that my experience is not unique and that many families have had similar experiences. It was with this in mind, that I decided to write a book with a composite of information. In the following, you will find anecdotal stories from other families and people who have made close observations of someone with Down syndrome, opinions on how best to encourage success in a variety of areas, the most credible and most current research on Down syndrome, and the indescribably beautiful photography of Kendra Dew. The stories have been told to Brian Skotko, who rewrote them in a singular voice while keeping true to the content of the original story. He is also responsible for combing the library at Duke University for the most current research, sharing it with me and enabling me to make the best selections for this book.

This book should be proudly displayed on a coffee table, for it is not a discussion on difference, but a celebration of joyful lives. The photography will make you smile with recognition of a shared moment, the stories will make you believe, the research will support that belief with fact, and some of the suggestions will help provide new insights into each child as a learner, an athlete, a sibling or a friend.

When a family has a child with Down syndrome, lives are changed forever. More than anything, a mother or father no longer has the right to be timid. It may be unfair, but it is true. You must advocate for your child. This requires stepping out of our own comfort zones for many people. What do you do when your doctor doesn't respect your wishes? How do you teach a child who learns differently? Does the church or temple you attend continue to meet the needs of your family? Is the youth sports organization accepting of your child? These questions will be answered in the coming chapters with ideas, exciting examples and documented research. The individuals with Down syndrome whom we have met in creating this book are inspiring, astounding and clearly NOT whom you have read about in clinical literature. These are vibrant members of schools, sports teams and society. These are people who play musical instruments, participate in worship services and inspire their coworkers to strive to do their best. These are people whom we are privileged to call friends.

The fabric of our lives is richer, the texture more diverse, the color palette more vibrant than those whose lives have not been touched by difference. Whether you are a parent, a teacher, a physician, a therapist or sibling, your life is enhanced by your belief in someone whose learning style is inherently different. Viva la difference!

— *Cynthia S. Kidder*

Since all children learn differently, sometimes we have to adapt our teaching. Jordan's piano teacher, Cindy, traced an outline of his hands in different colors during his first piano lesson. This tracing was large and just inside the front cover of his lesson book. The left hand was green, and the right hand was blue. When I came to pick him up, he showed it to me with great pride. I asked him why the hands were different colors and he answered: "Because the grass is always beneath the sky." In a simple modification to encourage learning, Cindy had come up with a memorable way to separate the treble clef from the bass clef in his mind. Translated to the notes he was about to learn to read, the treble line was colored blue, the bass line green. He always knew which hand played which score.

As Jordan's learning progressed, so did Cindy's accommodations. Some notes were written in for him. Always blue for treble, green for bass. Soon she was able to write in just the hard-to-remember notes; reminders so that learning took place before frustration set in. Now, almost three years after his first lesson, Jordan reads music. He plays the piano. The key is someone taught him! Cindy was not the first teacher with whom I attempted to enroll him. Indeed, piano began as one of the more painful chapters in Jordan's life. More honestly, it was painful for me as his mother. Three experienced teachers refused to accept a child with Down syndrome as a student. They would not even try. We were left with two options: give up or move on. Of course

we moved on and found a teacher whose basic belief is that all children are learners. Jordan learned to play the piano. I learned that when a teacher says she can't accept Jordan, she or he is probably making the right decision for themselves. Jordan deserves a teacher who relishes the opportunity to teach him. Cindy has learned as much from Jordan as he has from her. She delights in his accomplishments and she struggles for new approaches when he is stuck. When Jordan played "Happy Birthday" for Harper's twelfth birthday, our whole family was reminded of the joy of music.

— *Cynthia S. Kidder*

BAND OF ANGELS PRESS SURVEY

According to families surveyed by Band of Angels Press, 1 out of every 5 children with Down syndrome plays a musical instrument. For children older than 10, that number doubles.

One out of every 5 children with Down syndrome sings in a choir or vocal group. For children older than 10, that number climbs to 1 out of every 3.

Two out of every 3 children with Down syndrome like to draw and/or paint pictures. ✍

Artists

Sound waves in the water

OMAHA, NEBRASKA

"I'm going to be quite honest with you," said the talent scout to an over-crowded room of hopeful stars. "In fact, I may even hurt your feelings." Simply put, most contestants are never selected. For Leah Stodden, the opposite was true. She was chosen to be one of the 700 contestants from around the world to participate in a modeling and talent competition in Orlando, Florida. As her family would note, Leah worked hard to get there.

When only 2 months old, she began listening to her mother play the family's piano. At the age of 1, Leah had her own toy keyboard, and by the age of 7, she was already tickling the ivories. Her mother became her first formal music teacher. "Leah was very receptive and eager to learn new things," said her mom. "but after a while, I just wanted to try another teacher."

Piano, however, soon became a frustrating experience for everyone involved. "This is too hard," Leah would complain to her mom. The new teacher was rigid, and she became discouraged when Leah didn't progress according to the order in the piano primer. Finally, after many unsuccessful compromises, Leah went back to her mom for lessons and practiced her heart out. Within no time, she began winning awards. For five consecutive years at the Nebraska Summer Music Olympics, a competition that provides no special provisions for children with Down syndrome, Leah clinched the top prize for her waltzes, sonatinas, minuets and boogies. In fact, two judges gave her a certificate of distinction, an award reserved only for pianists who surpass even the highest level of performance. "I have given only two today," wrote the judge on Leah's score sheet, "and I have heard 50 kids."

Then came the invitation to perform at the National Down Syndrome Society Convention. Before an audience of 300 individuals, Leah played six solos and four duets with her mother. Was she nervous? You bet, but Leah managed to calm her mother down before the performance. Afterwards, the audience's applause was electric. "Leah just makes the music sing," said her mom. Everyone there seemed to agree.

So did the judges at the international competition in Orlando. Of the 700 participants, ranging in age from infancy to adulthood, Leah was the only one with a developmental disability.

During the modeling portion, she was also the only one to receive applause from the judges and the more than 2,000 individuals who came out to see the event. During the talent show portion, Leah played two piano pieces, and the audience's response was overwhelming. "It felt really good," said Leah, "I was so excited." But as of late her audiences have been reduced to one. "I enjoy playing for Andrew, my boyfriend," she notes. He's one of her biggest fans, and songs like "Rolling River" seem to be their favorite. "The song is really like sound waves in the water," said Leah. To Leah's family, it is also a song of triumph and hope, evidence that anything is possible with a shared belief. ✑

"Sweet throw kiss
from little Brandon
every Thursday
he knows what
is important in life.
I blow kisses back
to him
to give and receive
love in a whisper."

— Judi Cook, piano teacher of Brandon Churchill
a 5-year-old with Down syndrome
Bothell, Washington

A One-Man Band

GOLDEN, COLORADO

On the way to his sixth-grade band concert, Greg Hauserman told his mother that he would be playing a drum solo. "Of course, I didn't believe him," she said. Was he even good enough to play in the regular band? But, indeed, at the end of the concert, the band teacher announced that the final piece would be performed by Greg alone. And with his solo piece, he wowed everyone. "The whole audience just stood up and applauded," said his mom. "I was so shocked and so proud." Just imagine how proud she must be now. In addition to the drums, Greg, a 15-year-old with Down syndrome, also plays the piano, violin, clarinet, saxophone, guitar, banjo and marimba. Their basement is now Greg's studio and is even complete with a microphone for impromptu singing. Amazingly, though, Greg only practices once a week.

Nevertheless, those 90 minutes are electric as he and his music therapist turn that basement studio into a live concert hall. "When Greg was in fifth grade, I was reading about music therapy in a Down syndrome newsletter," said his mom. "It was the first I had heard of it." Since then, Jenni Lee, a music therapist has been coming to their home to develop a variety of skills in Greg. While she has made several adaptations to accommodate Greg's needs, she doesn't compromise the material. "You don't ever want to limit a child's capacity to learn," Jenni said. "So instead of saying 'let's pick up the volume,' you say, 'note the crescendo.'" And Greg certainly seems to have taken note. On the clarinet alone, he has a repertoire of 140 pieces. When he surpassed Jenni's level, she took him to see the principal clarinetist in the Colorado symphony. He worked on embouchure with Greg. At the end of the hour lesson, the clarinetist was amazed by the progress. "Greg sounded great," said Jenni. "No one has mastered the clarinet quite like him." Of course, there was a time when she would have doubted it.

"When I was in school, I never thought that I would be able to teach the clarinet to a child with Down syndrome," Jenni admits. "Now all the kids have surpassed what I initially thought they could do. Greg, specifically, is a weekly reminder of the pure joy of music: that joy of getting a piece exactly right for the first time or that joy of playing a favorite song over and over again." And that one-man band has no intention of stopping. "We're currently looking for a harp," said his mom. ✺

A Prize for the Pharaoh

KNOXVILLE, TENNESSEE

In 1983, the school system in Knoxville, Tennessee, questioned the usefulness of an arts program for individuals with disabilities. "You think your child's a Van Gogh?" administrators reportedly asked one of the parents. Evidently so. For that same year after the school provided the program, Margie Easterday, a 21-year-old with Down syndrome, won a national contest for her drawing of King Tut.

It began as a simple day. The art teacher asked her students to submit a drawing for a local contest. Students from all across Tennessee, both with and without disabilities, competed by drawing something of their choice. For Margie, however, the subject was never in question. She always had a penchant for King Tut. Just visit her bedroom, and you will find several books about the pharaoh stacked beside her bed.

In a two-and-a-half foot mixture of oranges and golds, blacks and whites, King Tut was resurrected. Margie kept the painting a secret. In fact, her family saw it for the first time when it was on display. "We were just amazed," recalls her mother. "To Margie, it was perfect, of course." And others agreed. "You wouldn't believe the number of art schools that wanted her to enroll!" said her mother. At the end of the day, Margie had won the blue ribbon for her painting.

It did not stop there. By placing first in the local competition, Margie qualified for the national competition in New York. Her painting again clinched top honors. The pharaoh soon became so popular that the Coran Gallery of Art in Washington, D.C., displayed it for a month and then purchased it from Margie so that it could be part of its permanent collection. Yet even as a part of an official collection, the painting has continued to accrue honors. Just recently, it won the National Scholastic Art and Writing Award and has continued to draw attention wherever it is displayed.

For Margie, painting will always be a way of expressing her feelings. She continues to draw and gives many of her new originals to family and friends. Her own mother, in fact, started a personal collection from the paintings that Margie has given her. "They're absolutely beautiful!" she said. "I cherish every one of them."

"One of my fondest and most vivid memories of Aunt Nancy was the way she would play the piano. She'd close her eyes and begin to play. Her hands would flow up and down the scales and across the keys in a way that would give my brother and me chills. The chord patterns sounded more like a concerto than the random notes that she was playing. It still gives me goose bumps thinking about it."

— Jim Westphalen commenting on his aunt, Nancy Ethel Wood
a 52-year-old with Down syndrome
Burlington, Vermont

A One-Way Ticket

COLDFOOT, ALASKA

"Up on the mountain there once lived a boy,

Down in the valley lived his only joy.

Late in the evening at the dawn of the moon,

Our young heart would swell to his old country tune."

To the people of Coldfoot, Alaska, that boy is Jeremy Bedingfield, a 17-year-old with Down syndrome. His favorite tune, "Yodeling to Molly," contains some ironic parallels. For one, Jeremy lives in the mountains where the temperature drops to -60°F during the middle of winter and climbs to 90°F during the core of summer. Approximately nine people call this place home; the majority of whom work at a truck stop for the Alaska pipeline. If you visit, do not expect to watch television shows or listen to radio programs because there are none. Instead, you will be entertained by something far more unique and far more captivating. Your heart will swell to the tunes of Jeremy.

"Jeremy learned to yodel before he learned to speak," said his mother. In fact, it is a talent that he continues to practice every day. Originally, he had learned the songs of his father, but now Jeremy's proudest accomplishments are the songs that he composes. At the post office you can receive your own personalized song.

Jeremy works there; but during his breaks, he likes to get out his guitar and strike up a new tune. According to his mother, the passers-by just love his humorous observations. But yodeling is not his only charm. In fact, he is an "imitation country singer" and has purchased more than one hundred CDs with his earnings. How often does he listen to this music? "It would be 24 hours a day, if he could," said his mom. And if you have an ear for country, you may recognize that a good portion of these songs come from his idol, LeAnn Rimes. Not only is he an official member of her fan club, but he has decorated his bedroom with her posters and calendars. LeAnn would likely agree that Jeremy has his own "One-Way Ticket" bound for success. He certainly adds meaning to her lyrics:

"Gonna climb the mountain

And look the eagle in the eye

I won't let fear clip my wings

and tell me how high I can fly."

The New Van Gogh

PARMA, OHIO

Ever since members of the U.S. Congress launched their annual high school art competition in 1982, more than 650,000 students have tried to compete for this national exhibition. Within the 10th Congressional District of Ohio, alone, nearly 400 students from 14 different high schools submitted artwork to Representative Dennis Kucinich for the spring 2000 contest. Just imagine a student's thrill after being selected among so many entrants! But Dennis Kucinich's 2000 awards ceremony proved a unique thrill. When contest judges announced that the first place painting belonged to Doug Forster, everyone was somewhat surprised to see a 16-year-old freshman with Down syndrome walk up to the podium to claim the prize.

Even his own mother was stunned. Doug expressed little interest in art at home and drew stick figures at best, according to his mom. So where did he develop such talent? "I think it comes from the fact that Doug has such a wonderful teacher," his mother said.

For five days each week for the entire school year, Doug created art for 47 minutes each day in art class. It was here that he developed a passion for Vincent Van Gogh. "I don't water the material down, and I don't change the vocabulary," said Doug's art teacher, Jerry Devis. Instead, the classes are "success-oriented." He teaches in incremental steps, allowing students to manipulate various forms of mixed media. For example, after teaching his students about Jackson Pollock—the legendary 20th century abstract painter known for his canvases of splotches, streaks, drips and dabs—Doug and his classmates were given boxes, marbles and cups of paint. In effect, they could create similar masterpieces by shaking the paint-coated marbles within the boxes. And like Pollock, every painting was different; for different students shook the boxes with different emotions.

When the time came for a lesson on color and expression, it seemed only appropriate to begin with an introduction of Van Gogh. "I showed a videotape of Van Gogh's life," said Doug's teacher. Then, he showed one of Van Gogh's sunflower paintings; and afterwards, he brought in some dried sunflowers for the students to observe. For Doug, this lesson was inspiring, and he has since imitated the artist's style in his own portfolio.

For the Congressional art competition Doug created his own sunflower painting. In an 18- by 24-inch montage of mixed media, three overlapping sunflowers shimmered in shades of gold and yellow-orange at the eye level of the observer. Doug began by pasting warm shades of colored tissue paper on brown wrapping paper. Using tempra paint, he added the petals. Using actual leaves collected around the school, he imprinted foliage along the base of the painting. Finally, Doug outlined his sunflowers in greater detail using various colors of oil pastels. "It was a brilliant interpretation of a brilliant season," said his teacher. But that's not all for Doug. In preparation for a class field trip to NASA, Doug created a celestial interpretation of the Sun, Mars and other planets after seeing a copy of Van Gogh's 1889 *Starry Night*. By the end of the year, he had assembled a portfolio of about 25 to 30 works—which explains why Doug's mother was stunned to receive the contest news. Except for a few drawings displayed around parent-teacher orientation time, all paintings are sent home at the end of the school year. According to Doug's art teacher, bringing home the portfolios at the end of the year is like bringing home a collection of emotion, hard work and pride.

After the Congressional awards ceremony, both Doug and his painting went on tour. Doug's parents took him to the Detroit Institute of Arts to see a Van Gogh exhibit, and his painting went to various malls and exhibits to be displayed. "Every child should have a chance to express their ideas," said Doug's art teacher. ✐

Kick off your Sunday Shoes

CARY, NORTH CAROLINA

Imagine going to watch your child dance in the city parade. She is anxious. You are excited. The day seems perfect. Now how would you feel if the dance instructor yanked your child out halfway during the performance? To Jenny Lowther and her family, the event was crushing. Even at the spring recitals, Jenny was placed in the back row. She received little attention from her teacher, and her mother was told that Jenny could not keep up with the other children. But, at the tender age of 11, Jenny started to fight back. When her dance teacher attempted to remove her from another parade, Jenny refused to budge. In fact, she continued to dance until the finish line.

"Jenny proved that she could do it," said her mother. "She accomplished this in spite of overwhelming and almost unbelievable prejudice from the dance teacher." But enough was enough. Her mom removed her from the program, and with the help of her older daughter, Kristy, she began scripting Jenny's own choreography. Several times each week, Jenny danced before household mirrors with the moves of jazz, tap and even ballet. Before long, both she and her younger sister, Shana, were performing before 500 people at the North Carolina State Fair.

After that, the audiences only got bigger. When Jenny's mom sent in a videotape of their "Footloose" routine, Jenny and her sister were selected to perform at the North Carolina Special Olympics Opening Ceremonies. Dressed in shiny purple outfits that were trimmed with silver sequins, the two strawberry-blond girls now "kicked off their Sunday shoes" before a crowd of 3,000 individuals. The dance was so popular that the girls were then asked to perform at the U.S. pep rally for the World Special Olympics. "It was great," said Jenny, "it was a total thrill." And for her mom? "It's the closest that I've been to heaven on earth," she said.

Musical Signs

Who says a 2-year-old is incapable of doing something incredible? During a 1996 Christmas Eve service, Lea Renee Stull, though not yet able to talk, "moved everyone to tears," according to her grandmother. At the time, Lea communicated with a collection of sign gestures that she had learned from her mother. When she was only 10 months old, "I'm hungry," "I'm thirsty," and "thank you" were all part of Lea's sign vocabulary. Within no time, the entire family started using these gestures with their verbal speech. "It was incredible," remembers her grandmother. "Through these sign gestures, Lea was able to communicate much earlier than normal children!"

At the candlelight service on Christmas Eve, Lea became particularly fascinated when a dancer used sign gestures as part of a liturgical dance. These dances—somewhat rare among most churches—are expressions of liturgical music, often performed by a member of the congregation. Typically, no one sings. Instead, they watch and listen during the performance. After the dance had begun, however, Lea's grandmother noticed that several of the choir members, who sat facing the congregation, had started to cry. At that moment, she noticed that Lea was following along to the music with the appropriate signs at the correct rhythm. In effect, she was singing while everyone else was listening. "I cried," said her grandmother. "It was just a very special evening."

RESEARCH:

I've Got Rhythm

Catchy rhythms are hard to forget. We tap to radio tunes, whistle to commercial ads and clap to gospel choirs. Even as small children, we begin to pick up on the many variations of patterned sounds. Are there any differences, however, for children with Down syndrome?

Two researchers at the University of Nottingham examined the sense of rhythm and time perception between children with Down syndrome and their nondisabled peers. Participants were asked to reproduce various rhythms, ranging in complexity, produced by a computerized program. Responses were collected using an electronic tapping device and accuracy was measured on a computer. Even the simplest interpretation of the evidence shows a "remarkable similarity" between children with Down syndrome and those without. In fact, children with Down syndrome rivaled the rhythmic abilities of the other children. Ninety percent of the participants with Down syndrome reproduced the computerized rhythms almost exactly, and statistical analysis showed no significant relationships with mental and chronological age. Children with Down syndrome have a normal sense of rhythmic discrimination.

Another researcher at Cleveland State University agreed. A group of 20 children between the ages of 8 and 13—10 with and 10 without Down syndrome—listened to tape recordings of various pitches, dynamic levels and rhythmic varieties. In the end, the children with Down syndrome perceived music identically to their nondisabled counterparts. Interestingly, however, children with Down syndrome significantly preferred music selections at the softer level more often.

Since music is an inherently stimulating tool for establishing communication and interaction, it is not surprising for parents to find a keen sense of rhythm in their children with Down syndrome. Just like everyone else, they will be singing in the shower, playing musical instruments and collecting favorite CDs. Music is a nonverbal form of communication, and children with Down syndrome both understand and respond to it. Frankly, who could ask for anything more?

Stratford, B. and Ching, E.Y.Y. (1983). Rhythm and Time in the Perception of Down's Syndrome Children. Journal of Mental Deficiency Research. 27: 23-38.

Flowers, E. (1984). Musical Sound Perception in Normal Children and Children with Down's syndrome. Journal of Music Therapy. 12(3): 148-154.

Can it really be? Jordy is 11. I recall so clearly the day he was born in Somers, New York. Perhaps the main reason that I recall vividly is because of the foolish way I reacted when I found out that Jordan had Down syndrome.

Cyndie, our daughter and Jordy's mother, lived in Somers at the time. My wife and I lived in Rochester Hills, Michigan. Grammy left for Somers for the birth of Jordan and I, Grampy, stayed behind to work. We are close with our neighbors, so together we were quite anxious for the news of the birth.

The phone rang early Sunday morning on the third of September 1989 and Grammy announced, "It's a boy." He weighed seven pounds, 10 ounces and was 20 inches long. "Mother and baby are fine." I prepared a large sign and placed it in the front yard for the neighbors to see.

Three hours later the phone rang and I was told there was a problem. Jordy had a condition known as Down syndrome. Here is where the foolish part comes in: My initial reaction was to take the sign down. Was I really ashamed to announce the arrival of our precious grandson because he wasn't perfect? The reaction didn't last long, only a minute or so, but how could I think that way? Of course, I didn't take the sign down.

I remember the time I first saw him and took my turn coaxing him to eat. From then through his first T-ball hit and his first bow following a piano recital, he has been the apple of my eye. Jordy has brought so much joy to this entire family that I actually feel sorry for families that have only "perfect" children.

I look back on that one foolish moment 11 years ago and feel so honored to have the chance to see life through Jordy's eyes. He has brought us all closer to understanding the really important things in life. He is a spiritual guide without even trying to be. Jordy is a perfectly charming, handsome, cool kid, and we would not have him any other way.

— *Raymond J. Waltenbaugh*

BAND OF ANGELS PRESS SURVEY

According to families surveyed by Band of Angels Press, approximately 9 out of every 10 individuals with Down syndrome listened to someone read a book more than three times a week between the ages of 2 and 5.

Approximately 7 out of every 10 individuals with Down syndrome used total communication (i.e., signed gestures with verbal speech) between the ages of 2 and 5.

Approximately 7 out of every 10 individuals with Down syndrome saw a speech therapist two or more times a week between the ages of 2 and 5.

children

Riding the wave

MOUNT LAUREL, NEW JERSEY

John Garcia does not wait for things to happen. He is a go-getter, a do-gooder and a high-hoper. "We never know what to expect from him," his mom said. "We've just learned to ride his wave." And what an adventure it has been.

When John was born in 1972 with Down syndrome, the physicians informed his parents that he would never be able to read. Now, Barnes and Noble Booksellers is his second home. "Chinese philosophy is interesting to research," said John. "I like to read Confucius." In his room, you will find multiple stacks of books about Chinese philosophy and martial arts. "When John said that he hasn't been to the bookstore lately, he's talking about the past two weeks," said his mom.

Physicians recommended that John be placed in an institution at least until the age of 4. Instead, he lived at home and was one of the first individuals with Down syndrome to attend a regular school in the county. His teachers felt that he couldn't handle a full day at school. He did. Much to their surprise, he consistently nabbed high grades. "Medieval history was great," said John. "I did research on different things like knights in armor."

His mother often worried about his constant respiratory congestion. She was surprised John took up the trumpet, an instrument that demands a lot of blowing. John excelled and was a player in the only New Jersey band at President Clinton's first inauguration parade. "When I attended one of John's first band concerts, I was amazed," said his mom. "I had expected to hear an um-pah band, but instead I heard something wonderful." John is particularly good at jazz. Ask to hear his solo of Duke Ellington's "Satin Doll," or the theme song to *M.A.S.H.* since, according to John, he "can play that one blindfolded."

A pediatrician worried that John would suffer from low muscle tone throughout his life. John recently earned a first-degree black belt in Tang

Soo Do, a difficult style of Korean martial arts that demands physical vigor and "spiritual meditation," according to John. "I didn't have too much of a choice. He wanted to take classes, so we enrolled him in an adult class," said his mom, "and just because he had Down syndrome didn't mean that he got any extra time off." Now, John's working toward a black belt in Kenpo, a softer and perhaps more artistic style of self-defense. He also recruited his dad and two of his friends to take the class with him. "My husband says it's hard," said John's mother, "especially getting that leg up." Fortunately, he has a good tutor. "I try to help him out a lot," said John.

"I was in opposition to John becoming an altar server at our church," said his mother. "You have to carry the crystal from the back of the church to the front." But John was the first in his class to serve. "Monsignor told me that we were buddies," said John, and for five years he proved to be one of the best servers. In fact, whenever a visiting priest said Mass, the usual clergy often relied on John to help the visitor out during the Mass.

"The last thing in my mind was for John to drive a car," said his mother. "One day he came home from school and showed me that he had signed up for an after-school driver's education program." Imagine the shock. But John persisted. "I kinda got on my knees and begged," he admits. And sure enough, he passed the written test on his own; and, after some practice with his dad, he passed the driving portion on the first try. "It was great," said John who has since driven himself to karate lessons and his own job interviews.

Despite what others may have thought, John became a bookworm, a scholar, a jazz musician, a martial artist, an acolyte and a driver. "I used to have brown hair," joked his mother. "But we have given up resisting a long time ago."🧠

"As parents, we often have to remind ourselves to allow Emily the opportunity to show us what she *can* do, rather than assume what she *cannot* do."

— Pegi and Bill Chamberlain, parents of Emily Chamberlain
a 7-year-old with Down syndrome
Chesterfield, Michigan

A Special Tomato

DOLGEVILLE, NEW YORK

My dad and mom had four children. The first three were healthy, "regular" people. Then I came along, a baby with Down syndrome. I had a hole in my heart, a big tongue and a wobbly head. As I got older, I also realized that I am a slow learner. One day it was bothering me that I was having a hard time doing my school work. I told my dad about this. He shared a story about when he was out in his garden picking tomatoes the year I was born.

Every year my dad grows a garden and loves to plant tomatoes. At harvest time there were Beefsteak tomatoes on a bush. When he saw a differently shaped tomato, it got his attention. It had a large, smooth, bright red enlarged side that made my dad want to pick it up and study the bump. It was so unique and looked so appetizing. At supper, that tomato was just as juicy and tasty as the others.

Even though I'm different like the tomato, as a person with Down syndrome, my family and friends love me even more and want to help me when I need it. My dad tells me that even though I have more difficulty learning than my brother and sisters, my lovable and outgoing personality and strong character make me just as special as they are. Guess I'm the "SPECIAL TOMATO" on the Bergeron bush. ✲

— *Carrie Bergeron*

"I often think back to the child the first pediatrician described to us . . . I am proud to say that my son proves him wrong every single day of his life."

— Amy Elliott, mother of Morgan Elliott
a 4-year-old with Down syndrome
Mayfield, Kentucky

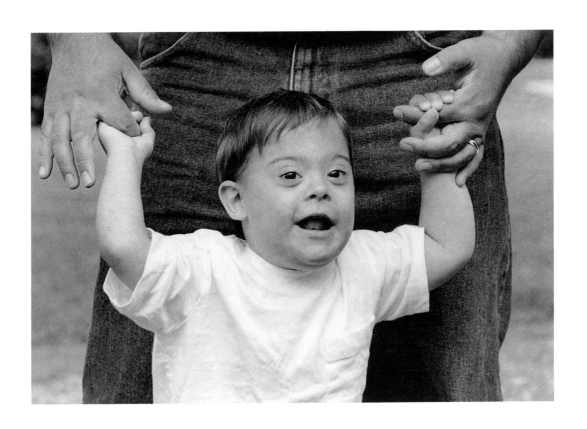

"With her courage, she gave us courage; with her love, we gave more love. We thank God every day that He gave Jenny to our family."

— Gloria and Vince Ferreri, parents of Jennifer Ferreri
a 21-year-old with Down syndrome, deceased 1995
Sterling Heights, Michigan

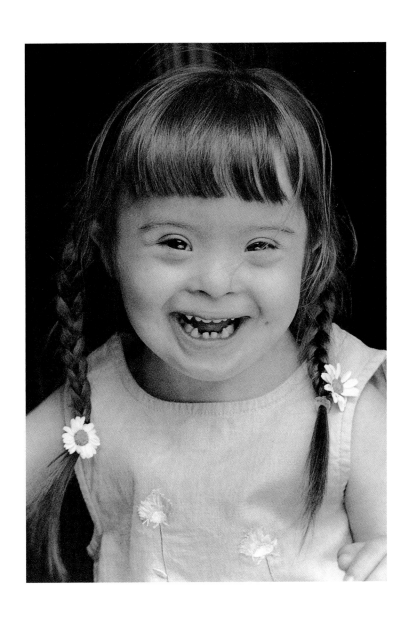

"To know Ashley is to love her."

— Michele Fedorka, mother of Ashley Fedorka
a 15-year-old with Down syndrome
Clover, Pennsylvania

"Tim's sense of humor, love of people and appreciation of the simple things in life have made our family more appreciative of those same things that we too often take for granted."

— JoAnn Herzberger, mother of Tim Herzberger
a 15-year-old with Down syndrome
Naperville, Illinois

"I have learned to appreciate the small things in life. I have learned patience. I have learned how to love, unconditionally. Thank you, my little miracle."

— Linda Kronmiller, mother of Eric Kronmiller
a 2-year-old with Down syndrome
Eureka, Montana

"He has taught us all the true meaning of love and of life and has given us all insight on how to live."

— Lenora Murad, mother of Anthony Murad
a 3-year-old with Down syndrome
New Hartford, New York

"Her unbridled compassion brings a new tear in our hearts each day because it breaks our hearts to think what the world would be like without Laurellen."

— Juliana Pickford, mother of Laurellen Pickford
a 7-year-old with Down syndrome
Picayune, Missouri

children

"I wish everyone could have a child with Down syndrome. They don't know what they are missing!"

— Jayne McDonough, mother of Lane McDonough
a 2-year-old with Down syndrome
Schaller, Iowa

"I see a child who places her love and concern for a fellow human over her fear of rejection and hurt. I see a child without judgment or prejudice. I see a child who places others before self. I see a child who perseveres. I see a child with courage. I see a child willing to take a risk to love. I see a hero. I see my daughter."

— Kelly Watkins, mother of Katherine Lowe Watkins
a 6-year-old with Down syndrome
Paducah, Kentucky

"I thank God that Molly was brought to us to enrich our lives."

— Darlene Whitis, mother of Molly Whitis
an 11-year-old with Down syndrome
North Branch, Michigan

RESEARCH:

A Call for Attention

Children demand a lot of attention. They need someone to read them bedtime stories, give them baths and cook them meals. But when your child is playing, how often do they look to you for help or approval? A researcher at California State University asked this question in a recent study on the social behaviors of young children.

Previous research had suggested that children with Down syndrome needed more attention from their parents in comparison to children without disabilities. According to the twenty children with Down syndrome who participated in this study, however, that theory may just be limited. Two groups of children and their caregivers were asked to play with various educational toys in a playroom setting. In the first group, children were asked to play with their caregivers. In the second group, children were asked to play alone, while caregivers busied themselves with paperwork.

In the end, children with Down syndrome played just as successfully and just as purposefully with the same number of toys as their nondisabled counterparts, thereby not supporting previous research claims that young children with Down syndrome persist less during play. In addition, these findings refute the claim that children with Down syndrome are less motivated than their nondisabled peers. When their caregivers actively participated in their play, both children with and without Down syndrome looked up at their caregivers approximately the same number of times. When the caregivers busied themselves with paperwork, both children called more attention to the task when they had successfully completed a puzzle or sorted different toys. In short, this research demonstrates that children with Down syndrome follow normal social orientation patterns. Although parent support is always beneficial, children with Down syndrome do not have any perceived social deficits that demand extra attention. "Young children with Down syndrome in their early years of schooling (e.g., preschool) may be able to work as independently and successfully as typically developing children on developmentally appropriate tasks," said the researchers. Furthermore, they suggest that children with Down syndrome can participate "in regular integrated classrooms in which adult assistance is offered only when sought."

Hughes, Margaret (1996). *Social Orientation Behaviors of Young Children with Down Syndrome in Achievement Situations: Another Look.* Italian Journal of Intellectual Impairments. 9: 3-12.

My son, Andrew, turned 12 this summer and has just entered middle school. As I picked him up today from his second day of sixth grade, his P.E. teacher asked me if Andrew would be interested in being an assistant manager for the school's football team. It was an exciting moment for both of us and didn't require much deliberation before we agreed.

As I reflect on Andrew's latest success, I am struck by the magnitude of his achievements. Is Andrew an exceptional child with Down syndrome? Yes. You cannot spend more than 10 minutes with this exuberant, physically motivated young man and not realize he is a natural athlete and fan for any sport.

Has Andrew grown up in an exceptional community to afford him such opportunities? Yes. He lives in a time and place where children of differing abilities are encouraged to develop and succeed. Andrew has been in inclusion since preschool. (Inclusion is the name of this crazy theory that kids do best in a less restrictive environment of their peers.) He attended his neighborhood Gymboree club as an infant. He took dance lessons at our local dance studio as a young child. Andrew has played T-ball, basketball, baseball and even flag football right alongside his classroom friends. He learned to swim under the tutelage of the assistant swim team coach at our community swim club. Andrew was accepted, encouraged and cheered on by coaches and parents who have no "special ed" training or experience working with "special needs" kids.

Does Andrew come from an exceptional family who expects such successes? Yes. We expect him to succeed in his own style and on his own time line. His father started taking Andrew to Detroit Lions football games before he could walk. His aunt bought him his first golf club when he was a toddler, and Andrew

has learned the rules and techniques of the game under her patient direction. For his twelfth birthday he played a round of golf with his uncle at his golf club. Andrew learned to ride his bicycle last summer after hours of encouragement by his most ardent fan, Grandma Joyce. She never stopped urging him to try "just one more time." Now Andrew regularly leads the family on our local bike trails.

While Andrew's life experiences have been exceptional, they need not be unique. Every life presents possibilities and potential. Our wonder-filled journey can either be spent celebrating the scenery along the route or grieving the path not taken. The potential for excellence in our lives is in each of us.

— *Sherry Viola, M.D.*

BAND OF ANGELS PRESS SURVEY

According to families surveyed by Band of Angels Press, approximately 1 out of every 3 children with Down syndrome older than 10 years old rides a bike without training wheels.

Seven out of every 10 individuals with Down syndrome older than 10 years old participates on an athletic team through Special Olympics.

Two out of every 5 individuals with Down syndrome older than 10 years old participates on an integrated athletic team.

Athletes

Hole-in-One Athlete

SWAMPSCOTT, MASSACHUSETTS

In October of 1997, the *Swampscott Reporter* boasted another golf triumph: "The Swampscott High School junior varsity gold team finished its season with a 37 - 34 victory over Winthrop. Jim Paige was medalist with 27. Seniors Lee Cooper, Jim Paige, Dave Shanahan and Jonathan Derr tied, while No. 2 player Matt Ingram won his match 6 - 2." Noticeably absent from the news article was the fact that one of the athletes has Down syndrome. But then again, why mention it?

Jonathan Derr can even beat his grandfather in the sport now. And that's not easy. "I was lucky that my grandfather bought me a little set of golf clubs when I could barely walk," said Jonathan. Each winter since Jonathan was 3, he has been flying to Florida for some tips from the family pro. "Jonathan's grandfather encouraged him to play golf," said his mother, "and they just have such a great time together." But their play was more than just fun. Very quickly, the family realized that Jonathan had quite a talent and enrolled him in golf schools, clinics, and private lessons. "When I was a kid, about 5 or 6, I was on the course

in a tournament for little kids. I hit the ball so far, and the next thing I know my grandfather found the ball in the cup," exclaims Jonathan. "A hole in one! I felt like the greatest." From there, things just got better. Eventually, he earned a spot on the Swampscott High School Golf Team.

In 1994, Jonathan entered the Massachusetts Special Olympic Summer Games and nabbed a first place victory in the nine-hole competition, oftentimes hitting the ball more than 175 yards. Doing so qualified him for the 18-hole, five-day competition in the 1995 Special Olympic World Summer Games. By this time, he had accumulated a cadre of fans—over 200 packed in three school buses to be exact. They all came from Camp Ramah, a summer camp in New England that Jonathan was attending. "The camp celebrated Jonathan for who he was," said his mother. The directors decided to turn the Olympic World Summer Games into an educational experience for all the other participants. So arrangements were made for everyone to attend the World Games.

"When Jonathan came into view, you wouldn't believe how loud those cheers were from the Ramah campers. I will never forget that sound," said Jonathan's mother. "You cannot imagine how it felt to have all these kids come up to thank me for giving them this opportunity. When you spend your time fighting for your child, constantly trying to open doors that someone is always trying to slam in your face, to have this unbelievable outpouring of love and support from *kids*, no less, was a healing moment for all of us." Jonathan took an impressive third place in that competition. Said Rabbi Michael Swartz, executive director of Camp Ramah, "There was such admiration and respect for him. He would be labeled by the rest of the world as handicapped, but for those of us who knew and loved him, Jonathon was a superstar."

Eunice Kennedy Shriver agreed, and Jonathan was selected to be the first Special Olympic athlete ever to be inducted into the National Jewish American Sports Hall of Fame in 1996. "Well done," she wrote in a personal letter to him. "What a victory for you and your wonderful family, supporting you all the way." He now ranks with such greats as Mel Allen of broadcasting, Red Auerbach of basketball, Sandy Koufax of baseball, Sid Luckman of football and Mark Spitz of swimming. "Truly, Jonathan is a young man for all seasons who has earned the respect of his peers and others because of who he is and what he has accomplished," said Annette K. Lynch, Senior Sports Training Manager for the International Special Olympics. Jonathan is grateful. "I have a very full and rich life, even with a disability," he said in his acceptance speech. ☺

"There she was, the smallest of all the sprinters. Those 50 meters seemed to go on forever, but one could see the joy in her face as she ran as fast as she could, smiling and laughing most of the way, but making sure she stayed in her lane and, most importantly, that she crossed the finish line."

— Tamara Spindler, mother of Kristen Spindler
a 9-year-old with Down syndrome
Stratford, Wisconsin

Number One Bulldog

BRIGHTON, MICHIGAN

It was a tense moment in the Brighton Bulldogs' locker room. Up until this game, they were undefeated. But so were their archrivals South Lyon. Everyone, sweating from the pre-game warm-up, knew that the winner had a chance at the conference title. They sat in uncomfortable silence. Suddenly, Derek Howes, a team manager with Down syndrome, walked to the middle of the room, clenched his fists and began to speak.

"He started low," said Matt Stone, one of the varsity football players, "but then his voice rose in such a crescendo of 'Gos,' 'Fights,' and 'Bulldogs,' that I thought his lungs would burst. His eyes squinted and his face turned red. He was more emotional than I have ever seen another human being in my entire life." It was the rally cry, the pep talk, the pre-victory cheer. Derek Howes had made it his mission to fire up the entire pack of high school athletes. "And when he was done," said Matt, "I was stunned. I wanted to cry and laugh and yell all at the same time." The entire team erupted into a deafening cheer that only a football team could produce. Charging Derek, they gave him a giant group hug and then ran out on the field. Needless to say, South Lyon never had a chance that night; and Derek Howes had earned a permanent speaking spot before every game.

Derek already knew the power of sports. Through Special Olympics, he was involved in basketball, baseball, soccer, bowling, golf, swimming, downhill skiing, and track and field. "He's my jock," laughs his mom. So when he entered the third year of high school, the assistant football coach asked him if he would become an equipment manager. "He jumped at the chance," said Derek's mom. Committed to the team, Derek rarely missed a practice. By senior year, he had earned an Ironman award, a signed football and a trophy during the final banquet.

Each accolade was hard-earned. For three hours, six days a week, another varsity athlete would pick Derek up, and they would drive to practice together. During workouts, Derek would help with drills, line up the equipment and assist where needed. He was valued and treated like another team player, and that meant wearing your jersey before a game at school (he was #18) and hanging out with the guys after practice (still to this day, he gets together with a group of friends to watch Sunday wrestling).

But by far, Derek's most important job was to rally the team with his speeches. He took them seriously and often rehearsed his talks in the shower. But before the Saline game, the last home game during his senior year, he practiced even more. "This time he spoke real slowly and got his point across about it maybe being the last regular season game for not only the players, but the managers, too," said Matt Stone. Players took note. "I learned one of the greatest lessons in life from Derek," said Matt. "He cares deeply about the game of football for the reasons that we too often forget. He loves football for the emotion, the thrill and the friendships."

"For the past eight summers one image has stirred a common emotion in swimmers and parents on both sides. The image of a young swimmer finishing her leg of a relay and being hoisted out of the water amid the congratulations and hugs of teammates. The inspiration lies in the fact that the scene is so normal. The fact that one swimmer has Down syndrome does not seem to matter, to Jenny Anne Lowther or her friends."

— Dana Wind, reporter for *Cary News*, on Jenny Anne Lowther
a 14-year-old with Down syndrome
Cary, North Carolina

Aerial Adventure

SPRINGFIELD, OHIO

Have you ever imagined what it would be like to coast about a hundred feet over the ocean suspended by a single parasail? Well, John Foster did; and when his mother suggested the idea during a family vacation in Acapulco, he jumped at the chance. He could imagine the thrill of being yanked off the ground as the motorboat sped away from the beach. He could almost smell the ocean as he raced above Mexico's shorelines, and he could see the mere specks his family members would be as he sailed at birds-eye view above the water. What he never imagined, however, was being refused because he had Down syndrome. "My heart sank," said his mother, "because that is the response that so many children with Down syndrome get." But John was determined to parasail.

He and his mother assured the worker that they would take full responsibility if anything went wrong. Finally after deliberations with the owner, John was permitted to sail. But parasailing requires some training.

After a harness is strapped to your body, you must learn exactly when to pull your cords. The first needs to be yanked when the boat makes its first turn. The second, arguably the most important needs to be timed at just the right moment so that you can descend upon the designated area. Pulling a bit too early means you will land in the ocean. Pulling a bit too late means you could land in an unmarked area further down the beach. You need to be exact when it comes to parasailing. "There were prayers for a safe return," recalled John's mother.

John has always loved a thrill. "He has a keen sense of adventure," said his sister, Beverly Edwards. "He loves activity." Consider his job for the park system, his cheering for the Red Sox, or better yet, the annual cookout he plans and hosts at his own condo. "My parents have exposed him to everything and anything," said Beverly. "They have taught him a love for life."

And a love for parasailing, too. John was smiling during the whole ride. As a matter of fact, he had attracted quite a crowd. "John's father and I had been standing in the back of the crowd to get a full view," said his mother. "Everyone applauded and cheered for John."

When it came time for him to land, everyone tensed up. This was the moment where nobody but John was in control. And he nailed it, landing on both feet. The original worker was so impressed he ran up to John's mother, "Congratulations, your son did everything perfectly." ❧

Finishing with Finesse

GREAT FALLS, MONTANA

Frankly, Jamie Darko's father was exhausted. For months, he had been running, pacing, even sprinting at times. But he wasn't racing against competitors, and he wasn't jogging toward a finish line. He was simply trying to teach Jamie, his son with Down syndrome, how to ride a two-wheeled bicycle. Perhaps, you, too, have helped someone learn to ride a bike. Remember the times you were unable to wipe sweat trickling down your forehead because you feared to let go? Or the times you ran an entire block with a body leaned against you, challenging the laws of equilibrium? Well, for Jamie's father, the situation seemed hopeless, and he gave up. Fortunately, Jamie did not.

One day while his father was at work, Jamie practiced with a cousin who was visiting for the day. They worked hard, and by the time his father had returned home, Jamie was peddling on his own. A few weeks later, he was riding around the neighborhood. By the age of 17, he had already competed in his first five-mile bicycle race. "Jamie knew that he would accomplish his goal," said his father. "I learned that if he starts it, he will finish it."

He continues to shock his family, even when it comes to the more unique sport of walleye fishing.

Jamie had been catching walleye, a Montana treasure, with his family since he was 3, but it wasn't until much later that they discovered his talent for fishing. One afternoon, he was out on the lake with his father and grandmother. Before they had baited up, Jamie yelled that he got one. "No, Jamie," his father told him. "You probably just snagged the net." Before they knew it, Jamie had reeled in a 24-inch walleye. After some celebration, Jamie's father and grandmother went to bait their own lines; but before they could finish, Jamie screamed again. "I got another!" This time it was a 26-inch walleye. "Jamie, are you trying to show your dad up?" his father jokingly pro-tested. Evidently so. Because before long, Jamie had pulled in yet a third walleye, weighing nearly sixpounds.

Neither his grandmother nor father had baited their lines. "He definitely showed us who the good fisherman was that day," said his father.

Jamie seems to have a special knack for every sport he touches. You name it, he's probably played it. Bowling, golf, basketball, swimming or even football—he's done it. And he has medals and ribbons to prove it. "Jamie's got awards hanging on his doorknob, his dresser, pretty much all over his bedroom," said his mom. Yet among all the athletic activities that these medals honor, one still remains his favorite—downhill skiing.

He began when he was only an infant. After his father finished his shift as volunteer ski patroller, Jamie would be strapped to a specially designed pouch on his father's back and, together, they would ski down the slopes. "He just loved it," said Jamie's father. And it still shows. For three months each year, Jamie participates in the Unified Special Olympic Program of Great Falls, Montana. In this athletic program, athletes with varying disabilities are matched with nondisabled counterparts, and they compete as partners. "It is such a growth experience for the nondisabled kids," said Jamie's mom. They learn how cool people like Jamie are, and they pass it on to their friends. Additionally, each person contributes an equal weight to the final totals. "They understand what winning means," said Jamie's mom. Everybody wants the gold medal, but they must compete together.

When the local competition begins each year, you can count on Jamie's parents being there to support him. "Every move he makes down the slopes, you feel yourself fidgeting," said his father. "It's as though you're skiing with him by his side." Over the years, Jamie and his partners have clinched first place honors at local competitions and have even snagged some medals at state games. But Jamie has set his sights on a new goal: to carry the torch for the International Special Olympic Games. ✸

Running After Makenna

SIGEL, PENNSYLVANIA

Late at night, the Truman family heard a creak from their front door. It was that slow, squeaky kind that can wake you up and give you chills. But in this house, it's a familiar late-night sound. It wasn't a burglar. It wasn't even Shadow, the family dog. It was Makenna, their 3-year-old with Down syndrome. She had taken off again and was headed outside to play. "Makenna loves to run," said her mom, "and she will run any time of the day." So the family got up, walked outside, picked her up and brought her back home. But nothing could stall their Energizer bunny.

When her dad came home from work, she ran to greet him. When her brothers were outside playing, she would race toward the woods. When she went to elementary school, even her four classes of regular physical education could not tire her out.

So when Makenna turned 5, her mother thought it would be a good idea for Makenna to run in the town's Little K event, a race sponsored by the local YMCA for 5- and 6-year-olds. The children had to race up a city block and then back.

It was quite some distance; and children with disabilities rarely participated. But when the announcer said, "Runners take your mark," Makenna was there with the best of them. Of course, the run was a bit farther than her usual race to the family pond, and as the other children crossed the finish line, Makenna had just reached the halfway mark. A YMCA volunteer ran out to Makenna and kindly offered a hand to help finish the race. Absolutely not! Makenna was determined to finish the race by herself. "No one seemed to move," said her mom. "Everyone began to cheer for Makenna as she ran the final distance with a huge smile on her face." She made it, and what a champ she was. "She wasn't by any means the fastest runner but she was persistent and proud," said her mom.

RESEARCH:

Striking Success

When 30 junior high school students from urban Minneapolis came to the local bowling alley, they all shared a common goal—to improve their bowling averages.

In this study conducted by researchers at the University of Minnesota, the athletes were assigned to one of three groups, each composed of four individuals with Down syndrome and six who were nondisabled. The first group of athletes were instructed to improve their group score by fifty points each week. The second group of bowlers were asked to maximize their personal scores in an effort to outperform their peers. Finally, each teen in the remaining group was supposed to improve his or her previous score by ten points each time. Respectively, these team structures simulated cooperative, competitive and individualistic environments.

After an eight-week bowling bonanza, the results were clear. Individuals on the cooperative team interacted at a significantly higher rate when compared to their peers in the competitive and individualistic groups. During a single game, the nondisabled bowlers in the cooperative group interacted more than 90 times with their teammates with Down syndrome. These interactions included verbal praise, cheering and assistance in handling the bowling ball. Only eight such positive interactions were made in the individualistic group, and less than four were observed in the competitive group.

Bowlers in the cooperative setting also seemed to like each other more. After the final week of bowling, each teenager was asked to rate his or her teammates. Athletes in the cooperative group both with and without Down syndrome gave each other significantly higher ratings than their peers had done on the competitive and individualistic teams. Even though individual bowling scores did not improve dramatically over the course of eight weeks, the participants on the cooperative team viewed the experience as both positive and enjoyable.

Interpersonal attraction, therefore, does not depend solely on performance. Teenagers with and without Down syndrome were able to form positive relationships, regardless of their scores. An integrative environment, however, is simply not enough. Only when an event is structured around cooperative goals can the members of an integrative team fully appreciate the rewards of athletic camaraderie. Clearly, athletes with Down syndrome can add an extraordinary richness to integrative sports.☞

Rynders, JE; Johnson, RT; Johnson, DW; Schmidt, B. (1980). Producing Positive Interaction among Down Syndrome and Nonhandicapped Teenagers through Cooperative Goal Structuring. American Journal of Mental Deficiency. 85(3): 268-273.

In the early days, when we knew less, we suspected Jordan would be devoted to his brothers, Harper and Kevin. We did not yet understand that he would be the super-glue for the whole family. Back then, we prayed that one of his brothers would include him in their home some day. Now we know that Jordan will likely live on his own in his adult years. We just hope that he chooses to live near one of his brothers and invites us to dinner often.

By having Jordan as a brother, Harper and Kevin have been given the gift of acceptance. It is a requirement for living in our home. Not just for them but for all of us. And, oh, how we all benefit.

Back in the preschool days, when the younger boys took baths together, I watched one evening as they played a game of "Walk the Plank" using Lego™ men and popsicle sticks. The popsicle stick perches on the edge of the tub and as each guy is told to walk the plank, he is marched to the end and ceremoniously plopped into the water. Harper had assembled the Lego guys using your basic head, torso, arms and legs. There was one exception.

One sailor had wheels where his legs would have been. I inquired about him, and Harper told me he was a wheelchair-user. Then, with no further discussion, Jordan placed this guy at the head of the line. When Harper shouted, "Roll the plank!" he too was plunked into the brine!

Theirs is a wholly reciprocating relationship. Just as surely as the Lego™ pirate received equal treatment, Jordan gets no special treatment. There is no sense of one-sidedness. Best of all, when you read the following stories you will see this is not unique. It is wonderful, but far more common than unusual. Not all siblings share the level of bond written about in this chapter and that's okay, too. Similarily, not all sibling relationships are the same when there is no Down syndrome. These are just glorious reminders of how full life can be for families of all compositions.✿

— *Cynthia S. Kidder*

Brothers & Sisters

Sibling to the Rescue

NORTH BRANCH, MICHIGAN

It was the middle of summer, and it seemed like a good thing to do. So Jeremy Whitis and his sister enrolled in a CPR and First Aid class at their local ambulance base. At first, some instructors were doubtful that Jeremy, a 17-year-old with Down syndrome, could pass all of the requirements. When it comes to lifesaving techniques, you cannot be very flexible. "Jeremy had to do it right," said his mom. And he did. Within no time, he had impressed the instructor, passed the tests and received his certification just like everyone else. But how often does a person use these techniques? For Jeremy, it was less than two weeks later.

What began as a normal day turned into a near tragedy. Jeremy's parents had left the house to run some errands, and the Whitis siblings were playing inside (or so everyone thought). Jeremy briefly stepped outside to enjoy some summer sun, and within minutes he heard a splash. The frightening kind where you sense something has gone terribly wrong. Jeremy turned toward the noise: his 2-year-old sister had somehow climbed onto the family's deck and jumped into their four-foot pool. She sunk right to the bottom. Without hesitation, he jumped into the pool, scooped up his sister and placed her on the pool deck. What exactly happened in those next precious minutes will always remain a bit of a mystery because it was quite some time before another sibling would come outside and find the two shaken, but okay, by the side of the pool. Though if you ask Jeremy what happened on that afternoon in 1991, he will demonstrate the chest compressions of CPR. Regardless of the specifics, he saved his sister's life.

His parents returned home shortly afterwards and immediately took their youngest child to the hospital.

"After I got the feeling back in my body, I was thrilled at what Jeremy had done," said his mom. "He is a true hero." The Governor, Senator and State Representative of Michigan agreed. Later that summer, they presented a Special Tribute, an award given to only three citizens of Michigan each year, to the same person who was once described by a pediatrician as "a child who would never accomplish much in life." Of course, that doctor couldn't have been more wrong. He probably didn't even realize that Jeremy was part of an extraordinary family.

Jenny, Katie, Tom, Molly, Josie, Brandon and Whitney are Jeremy's seven younger siblings in order from oldest (Jenny is 25) to youngest (Whitney is 2). The five youngest are adopted and have identified special needs. Labels never mattered too much to their mom and dad, who have been foster parents now for over 25 years. "I always just wanted to have a large family," said their mother. And amid all the spectacular stunts and miraculous rescues, what a thrill it has been! Simply put, the Whitis family is united in a simple belief: with love, all things are possible. ✿

"My brother and I will always be close. Nothing could ever come between our friendship."

— Alex Fitzgerald, age 9, brother of Tyler Adam Fitzgerald
an 8-year-old with Down syndrome
Fenton, Michigan

They Go Together

When the touring Broadway cast for *Grease* came to Cleveland, it only seemed natural for Kristin Skotko and her family to see one of the first shows. For quite some time, Kristin, a 19-year-old with Down syndrome, had been hopelessly devoted to Danny, the show's main character .

About 30 minutes before the show began at Cleveland's Playhouse Theater, one of the cast members came out and asked the audience to join him for a dance competition on stage. "Who in their right mind would go up on stage before thousands of people and boogie?" said Brian, Kristin's brother. At just that moment, Kristin yanked his arm and said, "Let's go."

"Absolutely not," said her mother, "You sit down." But Kristin was determined to dance. Besides, she had the aisle seat, so no one could stop her. "What was I supposed to do?" said her brother, "I got up and tried to get to her before she made it to the stage." The aisles were filled with latecomers, so by the time Brian made it to the orchestra pit, she was already on stage. "At this point, there were already some 20 individuals on stage. So I was thinking we could just dance in the corner," he said.

Brian joined her on stage. But the announcer did say it was a "competition." After the stage was filled, he told the contestants to dance their hearts out because if he touched them on top of their heads, they had to return to their seats. "Now I have to admit, Kristin is a pretty good dancer," said Brian, "But I was just saying to myself, 'touch us,' 'touch us,' 'touch us!'"

Here's the way it worked: each couple had about 20 seconds to dance; and in the end, the audience would clap for their favorite. So Kristin and Brian did a rather complicated swing move called the "pretzel." "Sometimes at home, we would just fool around and dance that step," said Brian. "But now it was for real." Well, the audience loved it, and they won the competition. Both of them took a big bow and were awarded official *Grease* shirts. Additionally, during the radio scene of the actual musical, the announcer incorporated Kristin's name into some of the song lyrics. "She was completely thrilled," said her parents.

But Kristin also taught her brother an important lesson. "In that single night, Kristin taught me never to be afraid of the unknown. Opportunities like that come around only once in your life, and you have to seize them. She didn't care what others thought; she didn't care about messing up. She cared only about fulfilling a dream. For that, she will always be my hero," said Brian. Wahooo, yeah!

Brothers & Sisters

"I don't know what I would
do without the feeling of having
Lora be the other part of me."

— Lisa Bouillon, twin sister of Lora Jane Kelly
a 35-year-old with Down syndrome
Murray, Utah

Between Sisters

PORTLAND, OREGON

Samantha Lee was used to a doctor's visit. By the age of 13, she had already had numerous surgeries. She had always been brave. "She has had so many medical procedures that, to her, it's just part of life," said her mother.

So when the time came for Samantha to have her blood drawn for another operation, it was no big deal to her. The lab technician, however, disagreed. "I could tell by the look on her face that she was quite apprehensive about working on a child with Down syndrome," said Samantha's mom. So the technician asked Samantha's younger sister, Shannon, a healthy and athletic dancer, to keep Samantha "entertained" during the procedure. She tried, of course. But when the first vial of blood began to be drawn, Samantha's sister lost some color in her face. At the second vial, she dropped to her knees, and by the third, she was flat on her back. Samantha, however, never stopped talking. "Don't worry," she said to her sister, "it's all over now. I'll stay here with you until you feel better."

This day was just another in the girls' long history of relying on one another. They have always been by each other's side.

On Tuesdays, they would go to church for weekly Bible lessons. On other occasions, they would make crafts in a Special Friends Club. Even during vacations, the girls would ask to share a bedroom, telling secrets that only sisters could understand.

But, perhaps, their sisterly love is most striking during the ordinary days at home. "Samantha is certainly an anchor," said their mom, "Shannon knows that she can always come back to Samantha for love, especially after a hard day." The two girls genuinely respect each other. They also listen to each other, and in the process, both of them have grown wiser. "My younger daughter has taught Samantha how to have fun," said her mom, "and Samantha has taught her sister how to appreciate the good in life." But when it comes to lab work, forget it, said mom. "My younger daughter takes after my husband, they both drop at the sight of blood." ☙

"Words cannot describe the love and admiration I feel for her. I am proud to call her sister."

— Tiffany Annelise Morrow, age 10, sister of Justice Kaye Morrow
a 2-year-old with Down syndrome
Hatch, New Mexico

The Knave of Hearts

AMARILLO, TEXAS

Picture the scene: A troupe of people come out on stage dressed entirely in black with their faces painted white. They speak with silent laughter and cry with muted sobs; they communicate with elastic limbs and nimble movements. They are mimes, of course. But for the audience in Amarillo, Texas, a secret can be found among those similar white faces. It is the whisper of two sisters and their mission of possibility.

Emily Dodson, now a 20-year-old with Down syndrome, had always wanted to perform like her sister, Marnie. For years, she had watched her older sister act in community theater productions and high school shows. So when the opportunity came for Emily to join a pantomime troupe for the Amarillo College Theater School for Children, she jumped at the chance to be on stage. Marnie was already a member. "It was great fun," she said, "and I wanted to support my sister's efforts." Their message beamed—accept me for who I am.

Audiences loved the act. Emily loved the stage. Within no time, she was performing with the regular community theater group and even nabbed a Best Actress Award from her acting class for her role as the Knave of Hearts in *Alice in Wonderland*. Soon she started attending summer drama camps and high school theater courses, despite the trepidations from home. "I was always afraid that Emily would forget her lines," laughed her mother, "but she never did. In fact, she was quite amazing."

And so, too, thought the people of Amarillo, Texas, who presented Emily with the Distinguished Youth with Disability Award in 1990. It was clear, though, that the award was a victory for both siblings. "I would especially like to thank Marnie," said Emily during her acceptance speech. They had always been a dynamic duo, but just to set the record straight, the Dodson sisters also have different interests (as they proudly point out). When it comes to Shakespeare, Emily's the Juliet and Marnie's the Miranda. When it comes to college, Emily roots for Eastern New Mexico University while Marnie rallies for University of Kansas. And when it comes to acting, Emily will use a script whereas her sister favors the bullet points.

Amid all these important distinctions lies a mutual feeling of respect. "Looking back I often wonder how my life would be different if Emily had not been given that extra little chromosome," said Marnie. "I believe that I might be left lying in a pile of self-defeat and completely self-handicapped if it were not for Emily giving me an example to follow."

RESEARCH:

Sibling Role Models

In the 1988 Oscar award-winning movie, *Rain Man*, Charlie Babbitt discovers that he has a brother with autism when his father bequeaths the family fortune to Raymond, his unknown sibling. Charlie locates Raymond and, in a road trip across the country, they develop a tight bond built on humor, trust and mutual respect. At the end of their journey, the two form a lasting friendship which values—rather than ignores—each other's idiosyncrasies.

Individuals with disabilities and their siblings seem to be bound by a special glue of understanding. For the brothers and sisters of a person with Down syndrome, the situation is no different. In fact, a researcher from the University of Washington showed that siblings can actually have a positive impact on the development of infants with Down syndrome.

In this study, six older siblings (ranging in age from 6 to 8 years old) interacted with their infant brothers and sisters who had Down syndrome (ranging in age from 16 to 41 months). In the first phase of this research, the siblings were videotaped playing with a set of toys in an unstructured setting at home. In the second phase, the siblings were trained to use social communication strategies to interact with their brothers and sisters. Strategies such as taking turns, elaborating on the infant's response, and follow-the-leader were used in the context of familiar games such as playing ball, blowing bubbles and playing peek-a-boo. One to three weeks later, another phase of unstructured play was monitored to observe the retention of these interactions.

The results were impressive. In the first phase of unstructured play, five of the six siblings already responded to at least half of the communications from their younger brothers and sisters. After the intervention phase, they responded even more frequently, providing immediate positive feedback and reinforcement. As a result, the number of spontaneous comments from the infants with Down syndrome increased; and four of the infants even showed increased complexity in their forms of communication. For all the siblings, these increases were maintained during the follow-up sessions.

In short, siblings can play an important role in the development of a child with Down syndrome. As shown in this study, they can even refine an infant's communication skills. And, as we all know, positive bonds formed during childhood can lead to friendships that last a lifetime.🧠

Richard, Nancy B. (1986). <u>Siblings as Communication Trainers for Prelinguistic Infants with Down Syndrome</u>. Dissertation Thesis at the University of Washington.

All children with Down syndrome not only deserve the right to sit in "regular" classrooms, but the right to be taught and expected to learn. They can and will learn. Our question should be: how much will we teach?

Jordan's speech therapy, provided by Jeannie at William Beaumont Hospital in Michigan, was extraordinary. It was also what I would call a pre-reading program. I describe this simply as a mother, not a speech therapist or an educator.

Jeannie initially worked with Jordan on muscle issues, making faces in a mirror, sucking through a straw, blowing bubbles—all exercises to develop those hard-to-reach oral motor muscles. He already made sounds but as his muscle control improved, so did his sounds.

Very early on, Jeannie worked on sentence structure. There would be no "me go in car" with her, it was "I want to go in the car." To accomplish this, she used a physical symbol for every word. "The boy is swinging" became a blue block representing the word "The;" a Little Tykes male figure, "boy;" a green block, "is;" a picture of a child on a swing, "swinging." And so with visual support, sentence structure became meaningful. The one-to-one correlation of language was clearly established.

When Jordan was about 4, I discovered my old business cards in a drawer at home. I took out a two-inch-thick supply and wrote a word on the back of each. "I," "love," "you," "Daddy," "Mommy," "Harper," "Kevin," "Grammy" and "Grampy" for starters. The small stack of cards fit neatly in my purse or pocket. When we had time, we pulled them out and used them. Harper, a year older, usually got the privilege of sequencing the cards into sentences such as, "I love Mommy." As Jordan's skills improved, we put in new words like "loves" which required him to see the need to change subjects as in, "Harper loves Daddy." The game was fun, it was meaningful, and we used it everywhere.

By the time he entered kindergarten, Jordan was a reader. He was a reader not because he is brilliant or because we, as parents, had specialized backgrounds. He was and continues to be a reader because his parents, grandparents and brothers believed in his ability to learn.

— *Cynthia S. Kidder*

BAND OF ANGELS PRESS SURVEY

According to families surveyed by Band of Angels Press, 3 out of every 5 individuals with Down syndrome know how to operate a computer.

One out of every 3 individuals older than 10 with Down syndrome reads the daily newspaper on his or her own.

Seven out of every 10 individuals older than 10 with Down syndrome read books on their own for personal enjoyment.

One out of every 2 individuals with Down syndrome go to school in a mainstreamed class.

Three out of every 5 persons with Down syndrome participate in school activities that are open to all students. ☉

Learners

Evolving Schools

SWAMPSCOTT, MASSACHUSETTS

Jonathan Derr thinks about big issues. So after learning about evolution in school, he challenged his Jewish mother. "Mom, do we believe in Adam and Eve or do we believe in the apes?" His mother thought about it and explained to Jonathan that evolution and the creation story are not mutually exclusive. In fact, she pointed out, many people believe in both stories. So upon hearing this, Jonathan paused, and after some reflection, he asked, "Well, are they Jewish apes?"

The teachers of Swampscott High School refer to Jonathan as an aggressive scholar. "He is an enthusiastic learner who is not easily flustered by assignments that he finds difficult," said Dawn Swimm, Jonathan's upper-level biology teacher. In fact, Jonathan is not afraid to challenge his own beliefs and that of others. "His disability became just a side note and is not what we first associate with Jon when his name is mentioned," said Dawn. "We learned that people with Down syndrome could be highly functioning." Unfortunately, not everyone knows that.

After grade school, Jonathan first enrolled in another high school where he took classes in cooking, woodworking and maintenance skills. "Administrators thought I was nuts to think he should be included in regular classes," said his mom. Jonathan was not permitted to take art, and his education was limited to the special education classroom. "I would often ask him, 'Whom did you sit with at lunch today?" said his mom, "He would just stare down at his feet."

So Jonathan switched to another school and became the first student with Down syndrome to be educated at Swampscott High School. With the help of an aide, Jonathan was fully included in classes such as child development, U.S. history, biology, physical science and media literacy. Within no time, he blossomed. During his senior year, Jonathan co-produced a 22-minute documentary video with his friend, Nate Rich, for their TV Production class. The video, entitled "Inclusion: Jon Meets His Expectations," nabbed the school's video-of-the-year award and won top honors from the American Association on Mental Retardation. More importantly, the documentary chronicled Jonathan's journey into the heart of his education, providing evidence that children with Down syndrome can *and should* be educated as aggressively and passionately as their nondisabled peers. "There is nothing in the last five or 10 years of our school's history, that I can think of, that I'm more proud of than Jon Derr's entry into Swampscott High," said Principal Peter Sach, "and I really mean that."

At graduation, Jonathan received nearly $6,000 in awards, including the school's esteemed Stephen David Johnson Memorial Scholarship. But, as his mother wrote in an editorial letter to the city's newspaper, there were nonmonetary gifts to be grateful for as well. "Somewhere along the way, you let Jonathan forget that he had Down syndrome and let him be a boy," she said. "This was perhaps your greatest gift to him." Jonathan currently lives in a dormitory with eight other young men and takes classes in money management and consumerism at a Cape Cod Community College.

"She believed in his ability to learn."

— Allison Leibig, commenting about the
second grade aide for her son, Tiej Leibig
a 10-year-old with Down syndrome
Whittier, California

All the Right Signs

GRAND BLANC, MICHIGAN

At first glance, you would think it was a typical day in third grade. All the students were seated in a circle, surrounding a teacher who had apparently grabbed their attention. Look a little bit closer, though, and everything may not seem as ordinary as you might have suspected. In fact, the teacher is only 3 years old and the students are talking with their hands. Cole Thomas Alvado knows how to capture the attention of a crowd.

According to his parents, Cole had mastered nearly 70 different signs by the age of 2 and began to supplement the gestures with speech by the age of 3. "When I found out that Cole was born with Down syndrome," said his mother, "I enrolled in a community education class on sign language so that I could teach him some gestures." His father especially believes that the signs were useful in developing Cole's speech. For him, signing was a way to communicate when speech would have been frustrating. "But as the signs developed, we definitely noticed an improvement in his speech," said his dad.

So, too, did the third-grade teacher who asked Cole to teach some signs to her classroom. "Cole was excited, of course, and the kids just took to him," said his mom. For one-half hour, he taught them the signs for colors and animals. They also learned the alphabet and, with the help of Cole's mother, the spellings of their names. At the end of that session, though, the third-grade students learned far more than simple gestures. They learned that everyone has something to teach, even a 3-year-old with Down syndrome. ❁

"She dazzled everyone at school."

— Pegi and Bill Chamberlain, parents of Emily Chamberlain
a 7-year-old with Down syndrome
Chesterfield, Michigan

A S-t-e-l-l-a-r Speller

LOVELAND, COLORADO

They were to learn about seeds that day. So Anne Brown's first-grade teacher brought in several types: apple, pumpkin, watermelon, you name it. The instructions the teacher gave the class seemed simple enough: copy the words off the chalkboard and match them with their corresponding seeds. But Anne hesitated. She seemed puzzled by the words on the board, and only began writing after some careful consideration. Out of curiosity, the teacher came to see what Anne had been struggling over and the source of confusion became clear. There was a misspelling on the chalkboard. But instead of copying the mistake like everyone else, Anne had correctly spelled "pumpkin." Embarrassed by the error, the teacher apologized to the class. "That's okay," Anne remarked. "We're all learning."

Call her the champion of letters, the queen of the alphabet. Ever since first grade, Anne, a 19-year-old with Down syndrome, has been her family's spelling primer. "We will often ask Anne for help with words that we are unsure about," said her mother. And where does such a unique talent come from? Her parents credit Anne's success to her passionate determination and a unique form of literacy instruction. Before Anne was 1 year old, her mother used the Doman flash card method which introduced various different words on large cards.

"We feel that Anne's spelling abilities developed along with this early reading program," said her mother. By 10 months of age, Anne could recognize her first words. Within a year, she could assemble those words into phrases. By the age of 3, she was already reading books and writing simple sentences. At minimum, Anne's literacy skills allowed her to be competitive in a regular curriculum. In fact, it wasn't uncommon for another student to turn to her for help with spelling. By the end of high school, she was already mastering orthography in another language. She had successfully passed an introductory class in Spanish and is currently enrolled in the next level at her local community college.

Perhaps the greatest test of her spelling skills came during one of her summer job interviews. Anne loves the outdoors and had applied for a gardening position. The interviewer was a bit surprised that Anne herself had completed the application. "You spelled all these words by yourself?" she questioned. Anne and her mother nodded in agreement. "I bet you can't spell Mary Poppins' favorite word!" the interviewer teased. "Of course. It's s-u-p-e-r-c-a-l-i-f-r-a-g-i-l-i-s-t-i-c-e-x-p-i-a-l-i-d-o-c-i-o-u-s," Anne replied.

"The kids in his kindergarten class treat him like a regular 7-year-old."

— Diane Kenyon, aunt of Ben Smithwick
a 7-year-old with Down syndrome
Phoenix, Arizona

"Our daughter, Kate, can make going to the bookstore a major adventure. She can teach you how to smell, feel and almost taste the excitement of books!"

— Karen Matrille, mother of Kate Matrille
a 14-year-old with Down syndrome
Oakland, Michigan

"I know that Taylor has opened a lot of eyes and minds in his regular education classroom. For that, he is a hero."

— Joann Spence, mother of Taylor Spence
an 8-year-old with Down syndrome
Romeo, Michigan

RESEARCH:

Citizens of the Classroom

When Isaac Johnson, a 4-year-old student with Down syndrome, entered Shayne Robbins' pre-kindergarten classroom, he already had a penchant for Max, the lead character in Maurice Sendak's *Where the Wild Things Are*. For years, Ms. Robbins had been asking her students to make panoramas for the story. After realizing that such a task may be too difficult for Isaac, she instead asked her class to develop a play based on the book. Although Isaac could not yet speak, he loved to pretend and had a fascination for drama. So the students created the scenery, costumes and dialogue. Isaac was a natural for the lead role of Max. When it came his turn to speak, he pointed to a communication board, and a classmate read the line to the audience.

Recently, a researcher from the University of Northern Iowa followed the lives of 10 students with Down syndrome across 12 classrooms over a two-year period. In his study, he notes that two broad definitions of literacy exist within classrooms. The first defines literacy as a linear curriculum that requires students to conform to a sequence of technical skills. The second, like that within Ms. Robbins' class, defines literacy as an evolving web of relationships connecting students, teachers and classroom materials. Ms. Robbins had altered the context of her lessons in order to include Isaac as a full citizen within her classroom.

For students with Down syndrome who were in a classroom of conformity, however, the results were far less encouraging. Joanna, a second-grade student with Down syndrome did not yet speak, formed a fist to grasp her pencil and often tore up her indecipherable papers. As a result, she was separated with four peers in a "print awareness" group where she listened to an assistant read a book and colored in pictures from the story. After a mere observation, however, the researcher noted that on several occasions, Joanna was able to articulate the final word in a sentence, suggesting she was able to read. Unlike Isaac, her capabilities were being undeveloped because she did not fit a stratified literate social structure.

Interpreting literacy as a web of relationships reconceptualizes Down syndrome "from a traditional context of global intellectual deficiency to one in which each child is recognized as uniquely valuable to the classroom community." Physical restructuring of the classroom, however is not enough.

Educators must redefine literacy from a mastery of subskills to a tool for communication. When they do so, teachers will have "turned written language into a path students might choose to solve problems, accomplish learning goals, express emotions, empathize with peers, gather and convey information, form friendships and resolve conflicts."

Kliewer, C (1998). Citizenship in the Literate Community: An Ethnography of Children with Down Syndrome and the Written Word. Exceptional Children. *64(2): 167-180.*

Arriving early for my volunteer shift at the elementary school, I found Jordan's class still at recess. No one noticed me as I observed their play. Jordan and three other boys were playing "It." Ben, a big kid, seemed to be in charge. Remember, size is power in the first grade. Watching, I was bothered to see that Jordan appeared to be "It" for life. No matter who he tagged, he was once again "It." As I got closer, I called out to Ben. Chatting with him (and possibly trying to manipulate him) I commented on how different this was from the game of tag I had played as a child. I also told him how reassuring it was to me as a mother to see him playing with my son, since I knew he would never take advantage of Jordan. Ben looked around in a guilty, uncomfortable way and then called out, "Hey Billy, you're It."

I walked into the school feeling I had accomplished something — a lesson on equality, fairness or diversity. Then Jordan spotted me and, face flushed from running, blurted out, "Guess what I did at recess? I got to play "It" with Ben, Billy and Mike!" Only then did I realize that my interference in their regular childhood play had far more to do with my needs than Jordan's. Jordan never minded being "It." He was just happy to be in the game.

That day on the playground was over four years ago. Billy, Ben and Mike continue to be friends of Jordan's to this day. How grateful I am to have learned to trust more so early in his life!

Even when the friendship doesn't look like we expect, there are some powerful relationships developed between young people with Down syndrome and their friends.

— *Cynthia S. Kidder*

BAND OF ANGELS PRESS SURVEY

According to families surveyed by Band of Angels Press, 1 out of every 5 children with Down syndrome talk on the phone with friends more than three times a week. For children older than 10 years of age, that number doubles.

One out of every 3 children with Down syndrome over the age of 10 years of age will write an e-mail on a regular basis.

Two out of every 3 children with Down syndrome over the age of 10 have a boyfriend or girlfriend.

Friends

The Odd Couple

LYNDEN, WASHINGTON

Becky Icenhower and Fran Armintrout are proudly different. The former likes chicken; the latter prefers fish. One is an impeccable organizer while the other is a confirmed slob. And while Becky can be the quiet pleaser; Fran can be the assertive curmudgeon. Even when it comes to the holidays, there are distinct preferences: Becky loves Halloween, and Fran likes Christmas. So how is it possible that this pair have shared an apartment for more than six years? The secret lies nestled in their common dream of independence.

"When Becky was 3," said her mom, "she stealthily made her way out of her crib from her afternoon nap. Before I had realized that she was missing, Becky had already walked down the street, entered the kitchen of a stranger and asked for a cookie." Out of panic, the surprised owner of the house phoned the police. That, of course, didn't stop the young escape artist. Just a few months later when the family moved to a different state, Becky managed to climb over the backyard fence without anyone noticing. She again walked a couple of blocks before a concerned neighbor phoned the police. "My 3-year-old had a police record in two states," laughs Becky's mom. Call it curiosity, cleverness or just healthy tomfoolery, but young Becky Icenhower was always on a mission.

The Armintrouts knew Fran was outgrowing their home after she moved to their basement. "All her siblings had moved out," said her mother, "so Fran wanted some independence, too." Furnished with a desk, TV, bath, bed and family room, the basement seemed like a nice compromise. Fran would "visit" her parents for dinners but spent the majority of time watching TV or making rugs in the basement studio. Quickly, she became lonesome.

"Fran had needs that we were not fulfilling," said her mother. "She needed a peer."

That turned out to be Becky. The two met through Cascade Supported Living, a Christian organization dedicated to providing assistance for persons with developmental disabilities.

In 1994, Becky and Fran, both of whom have Down syndrome, moved into a two-bedroom apartment. "Oftentimes, the general public thinks that all people with disabilities look and act alike," said Tanya Heutink, Program Director for Cascade. "Becky and Fran are almost complete opposites." As part of the program, each of the girls were assigned to an advocate and given help to make their new living arrangement work. At first, the girls met frequently with their advocates, discussing communication skills, sharing of resources and respect for each other's differences. Now, the advocates stop by only once or twice each week, helping to plan menus, sort out finances and provide occasional transportation. Like so many friendships, Becky's and Fran's differences have only made their relationship stronger. "Becky has definitely taught Fran how to be a bit neater," said Valeen Mulder, Fran's advocate. "And Fran has taught Becky how to be more assertive," said Becky Van Hofwegen, Becky's advocate. Together, they have grown and flourished in their common goal of independence. ☺

"He was an asset, and he knew it."

— Stacey Hayes, camp counselor for "Space Jam"
a 16-year-old with Down syndrome

Madame Butterfly

BRENTWOOD, TENNESSEE

Most people in Brentwood, Tennessee, agree Katie Ashley throws the best parties. Over 70 guests showed up for her 18th birthday bash and Katie dazzled. Her long straight black dress and sparkling jacket covered only one secret—Katie had to wear tennis shoes because of a painful disease that developed in her legs at age 7. Frankly, though, it seemed to be the style that evening. When her high school friends showed up for the party in long dresses, they, too, had worn their tennis shoes.

"Katie is a social butterfly and has a lot of peer tutors in her school who have become her friends," said her mother. "She's never let the fact that she has Down syndrome get in her way." Peer tutors are students who volunteer to help individuals in special education classrooms. For Katie, they have become friends. Take, for instance, Brandi, a 16-year-old tutor who picked up Katie one evening, took her shopping at the mall and then went with her to see a movie. Consider Melissa, the daughter of a teacher at Katie's school, who took Katie out to dinner and then invited Katie to her house for a sleepover. The number of phone calls Katie makes in an average week is a sign of her rich social life.

She's also a "hormonal nightmare. Just yesterday she was flirting with my hairdresser," laughs mom. And ever since the middle school Valentine's dance, Katie seems to "fall in love every couple of months," as her mother puts it. Prom was no different. After leaving her elaborate pre-prom party, Katie ran into a previous beau and danced the night away. "A couple of regular education boys also asked her to dance," said her mom. "She really thought she was something and danced until her legs wore out, and she had to be carried to the car."

"Katie has taught us all so many lessons," said her mom. "I had expected her to die before the age of 15. I expected her to be a vegetable after reading the literature on Down syndrome in the hospital." But the young Britney Spears fan has shown her family, her school and her community that she intends to grow up just like everyone else.

"Adam decided he wanted to go to his Homecoming dance and wanted to ask his friend, Kristin. She was absolutely thrilled! She called her sister at home and started planning her outfit. We took Adam shopping for a sports jacket and slacks and, for once, he didn't mind trying on clothes. They were just like everyone else, dancing and enjoying the evening."

— Jeanne Henning, mother of Adam Henning
a 20-year-old with Down syndrome, commenting
on his date with friend, Kristin Skotko
also a 20-year-old with Down syndrome
North Royalton, Ohio

Perfect Strangers

SYRACUSE, NEW YORK

For Julie Tennant, a 5-year-old with Down syndrome, the day started with another opportunity to ride in the front seat of the shopping cart as her mother stocked up on their weekly supplies at the local grocery.

When were in the check-out line, a homeless man walked through the front door of the store. He was gross, said Julie's mom. "His hair was so dirty and greasy that it clumped together." The man came wrapped in a wrinkled tan trench coat and wore a hat too dirty to make out its original color. "He obviously hadn't shaved in days and probably smelled," recalls Julie's mom, "but I wasn't going to get near to find out. I thought to myself how unnecessary this was. Syracuse has one of the top rescue missions in the country. He could at least take a bath and look presentable."

She took Julie out of the cart, preparing to leave. But as soon as Julie was placed on the ground, she took off right toward the man with her arms outstretched. He quickly bent down and picked her up. "She snuggled into his disgustingly dirty neck," said Julie's mother. "My heart panicked as I ran over to him."

"Excuse me, this is my child," said Julie's mom as she gently, but quickly, snatched Julie back. But then, all of a sudden, she stopped.

It was a moment she can still picture some 19 years later. The man, tears swelling in his eyes, turned to her and said, "Lady, I can't remember the last time anyone wanted to hold me."

Sometimes it takes a child to remind us how privileged we are. "Julie saw hurt and hugged it," said her mom, and Julie, has never stopped hugging. She is grown now and works four hours each day at Penny Curtiss Bakery. She and her mother have also volunteered for the Syracuse Rescue Mission for the past 10 years. It is here that she often encounters people similar to that homeless man she once embraced. And what ever happened to that man? "I don't know," said Julie's mom, "but I've been praying for him for 19 years. Both he and Julie remind me of the Bible passage:

'Do not forget to entertain strangers, for by so doing, some people have entertained angels without knowing it.'" (Hebrews 13:2)

Friends

"Tiej is a good friend to all of us."

— Raul Padilla, third-grade classmate of Tiej Liebig
a 10-year-old with Down syndrome
Whittier, California

Heart and Soul

MURRAY, UTAH

One the eve of their 33rd birthday, Lisa Kelly Bouillon's twin sister, Lora Jane Kelly walked into their parents' bedroom and had a heart failure. "My mother started screaming," Lisa recalls, "and my father immediately called 9-1-1." Lora, the twin with Down syndrome had struggled to breathe, and collapsed to the ground, unconscious. "We started giving her CPR, but my sister's eyes were just rolling," said Lisa.

Over the next five days, her entire family remained in vigil at Lora's hospital room. "On the second night, I held hands with her the whole night. I just kept making sure that her chest was going up and down," Lisa recalls. But, Dr. George Veasy, Lora's cardiologist for 26 years, comforted the family and assured them everything would be okay.

He was right. Within three weeks, Lora was back to normal, solving her word search books, making scrapbooks and "being as meticulous as ever," as her mother would say. But this event would later offer Lora a special opportunity. A year later she received a call from the American Heart Association asking if she would give a speech at an awards ceremony for Dr. Veasy.

Lora was thrilled and immediately agreed. She adored Dr. Veasy, or Uncle George as she called him. So at the annual Heart Ball, Uncle George, Utah's first board-certified pediatric cardiologist, would receive a lifetime achievement award, and Lora Jane Kelly would be one of the program's keynote speakers.

"Anytime I was sick, I called Uncle George, and he was right there for me. It didn't matter what day it was or what time it was," Lora began. She had practiced this speech for nearly two months and delivered it without flaw. "Two years ago I had heart failure," she continued. "Uncle George was retired at the time, but he made a special trip to the hospital to see me and to make sure I was taken care of. He is a great doctor and a true friend."

When Lora finished her speech, she had honored Dr. Veasy—and moved the 400 guests in attendance to a standing ovation. ❀

"My dream for peace is that all people can be friends. Anybody can be any color. Being different is okay. I love everybody."

— Mollie Rose Tew
an 11-year-old with Down syndrome
Holly Springs, North Carolina

Friendship

Friendship is caring and understanding in many ways.
Friendship is doing things with each other, sharing
secrets, sharing problems and helping each other.
Friendship is a special feeling that makes me happy.
A close friend is someone that helps you with
problems and really cares about you.

— Written by Rachel Keplinger
a 14-year-old with Down syndrome
Marquette, Michigan

RESEARCH:

In Good Times and Bad Times

Children today always seem to be "It." At the local playground you will find a dozen children racing around the jungle-gym in a never-ending game of tag. At the local swimming pool a child will try to catch his friends in a game of Marco Polo. Even in your own backyard, a child probably searches for friends in a game of hide-and-go-seek. Although your child may run up a slide backward, hold his or her breath underwater and hide among the bushes to avoid being "It," a research review in the early 90's argues that such play is both healthy and critical.

According to a researcher at the University of Washington, children as young as preschoolers need to engage in active play. In fact, establishing positive peer-relationships during the preschool years is a developmental milestone, "one that has important implications for children's cognitive, communicative and overall social development." For children with Down syndrome, the situation is no different. In fact, structured play may be even more important.

Early interactions with friends introduce children to a series of social tasks such as gaining entry into peer groups, resolving conflicts and maintaining play. From these situations, children then develop social strategies that can later help them achieve their own interpersonal goals. In short, children with Down syndrome should be encouraged to play among peers with and without disabilities. Doing so will foster social strategies that can last a lifetime. These strategies may include learning to negotiate during a dispute, dealing with one's emotion and valuing companionship.

Yet, should we ever meddle with the basics of child's play? Structuring children's peer relationships may be healthy at an early age, according to this research. Teachers can help, too. Appropriate interventions should incorporate the essential strengths of children with Down syndrome, particularly their skills in drama and other forms of representational play.

The results are in: Encourage your children to form friendships. Besides, being "It" only means you get to tag someone new.

Guralnick, Michael J. (1993). Developmentally Appropriate Practice in the Assessment and Intervention of Children's Peer Relations. TECSE. 13(3): 344-371.

Much about this chapter has been difficult. Choosing a title for it, selecting photography and stories, and writing this introduction. This is a challenge for reasons unique to Down syndrome. You see, when one has a child with Down syndrome, many people say seemingly nice things, like "they're always so happy" and "they are closer to God" and finally, "they are such angels." As any parent knows, no child is always happy. Any parent of a child with Down syndrome knows that children with Down syndrome are as unique as other children. Lumping all kids with Down syndrome in one category is not just inaccurate, it is simply ridiculous.

My very dear friend, Sherry, and I belong to the same church and the same summer swim club. Her sons are 12 and 8; mine are 19, 12 and 11. Sherry's 12-year-old has Down syndrome, as does my 11-year-old, Jordan. Over the years she and I have shared many general parenting experiences, as well as the unique aspects of raising children with Down syndrome. Best of all, we share a rather wry sense of humor and tongue-in-cheek sassiness.

Two summers ago, shortly after Sherry and her family joined the swim club, she and I were frequently annoyed and amused at the number of times our boys were confused with one another. Andrew is a head taller than Jordan and has short, light brown hair and a very athletic build. Jordan is slight, very narrow through the waist and wears his bright blonde hair in a longish surfer cut. Regardless, I was often approached in discussion about Andrew, and Sherry was praised for Jordan's participation on the swim team.

The day of the swim team picture, Jordan remembered to wear his team suit and reminded his brother to do the same. We arrived early, and Jordan took his place in the front row of 200 swimmers. I sat down to read a book and relax, but was interrupted by a concerned mom who wanted me to put Jordan in the picture. "He is in the front row," I assured her, but she insisted he was sitting under an umbrella elsewhere. I pointed him out to her, but she insisted I check out the boy under the umbrella. Of course, it was Andrew. As a nonmember of the swim team, he was politely sitting out the photo session.

Just weeks later, Sherry's boys and mine were participating in a church musical together. During the final performance, Jordan was absolutely angelic. He walked carefully in his Moses-style robe and sandals. He did all the right dance steps and sang with cherubic intensity. Andrew had a little more difficulty with the cherubic expectations. He twirled the rope that tied around his robe and came precariously close to lifting his robe so high as to reveal some critical body parts. As the parent helpers, Sherry and I watched the end of the performance from the vestibule. She smiled and even laughed aloud at some of Andrew's antics. I admired her ability to enjoy the whole performance rather than be critical or embarrassed about his rambunctious behavior. When I mentioned that to her, she laughed and said: "I was just thinking that 50 percent of the congregation thinks he is your son, and mine is the angelic one!"

— *Cynthia S. Kidder*

BAND OF ANGELS PRESS SURVEY
Approximately 7 out of 10 children with Down syndrome pray on a regular basis.

Angels

In the Arms of the Angels

NORTH MYRTLE BEACH, SC

When Jeremy Williams was 18 years old, he participated in a Confraternity of Christian Doctrine (CCD) class with eight other nondisabled high school students at his church. These weekly sessions gave teenagers an opportunity to learn more about Christ through studies of the Bible and church traditions. Jeremy's mom happened to be the teacher that year and during a lesson on the lectionary, Jeremy put his head down and went to sleep. "I didn't really understand what it was about," said Jeremy, "and I didn't want to go back." So Jeremy asked his mother if they could start a new class for individuals with disabilities. And so they did.

Jeremy and about seven other young adults with varying disabilities formed the first of such classes for the Diocese of Raleigh. "They had wonderful discussions about morality," said his mom, "and they talked about issues that concerned them—issues about sex, drugs and behavior." They also studied the stories in the Bible that mattered most to them—parables of Jesus helping people walk, see and talk again. "Jesus cared about the handicapped," said Jeremy.

But Jeremy's spiritual journey neither began nor stopped with his CCD class. He gave his first Confession to a priest at the age of 7 in his bedroom and by the age of 8, he became the spotlight of the church community when he received his first Communion. About 300 teenagers had just returned from a spiritual retreat, and the grand finale was Jeremy's First Communion. "It was the first time that I could talk to [God] inside of me," Jeremy said in one of his own prayers.

The church community was equally excited to see Jeremy become an altar server. Sure, it was difficult at first. He fell a couple of times and even dropped the hosts once, but with encouragement from his pastor, Jeremy soon became the admired acolyte. "The comments we got from everyone were 'It means so much to me to see Jeremy as altar server,'" said his mom. Later, when Jeremy was a bit older, he became an usher.

Jeremy also did a lot for the surrounding community. As a volunteer at Catholic Outreach, he distributed food and clothing to the homeless. As Santa Clause, he helped distribute presents to small children, and as a volunteer at a local Lutheran Church, he brought new meaning to the word "ecumenism." Now, Jeremy lives on his own in a beach house. He raises money for individuals with disabilities through his membership in the Knights of Columbus. As a third-degree knight in the Holy Name Society, he prays for those in need. "I have Down syndrome and that's special to God," he notes. "I think God put me here to love everyone."

It seems all too appropriate, then, that Jeremy took his Confirmation name from St. Francis of Assisi. He certainly seems to have lived the prayer:

"Lord, make me an instrument of your peace,
Where there is hatred, let me sow love,
Where there is injury, your pardon, Lord,
Where there is despair, let me bring hope,
Where there is darkness, light,
And where there is sadness, forever joy." ❁

"For the first few months of his life, I daily questioned God: Why? What did we do? Why is He doing this to us? But, as always, God is soooooo right!"

— Miriam Campbell, mother of Damon Campbell
a 34-year-old with Down syndrome
Darlington, South Carolina

Picturing a Deacon of Love

FENTON, MICHIGAN

When he was about 31 years old, Rick Stanfill drew a cluster of stick figures on a sheet of paper. To most people, it would have been a mere scribble, perhaps even a piece of trash. But to Susan Snedeker-Meier, pastor at the Westminster Presbyterian Church, the drawing was an "incredibly complex reasoning of time and self." In the center of the drawing, three adults were holding a baby. Behind them was a row of people wearing masks, and in the upper right hand corner was a mysterious figure with wings. "I asked Rick what it was about; and, together with his mom, we figured it out," she said. Rick had drawn his baptism.

When Rick was born with Down syndrome, doctors feared that he would not live past the age of 2. As a result, he was baptized immediately. The row of people in his painting, then, were actually the doctors wearing their surgical masks. His mother and father were two of the three people that were holding Rick as an infant. But as for that third person? "Well, when we were discussing the drawing, Rick's mother remembered there was another friend of the family present at the time," said Susan, "but Rick had no way of knowing this." Perhaps, then, it was the guardian angel in the upper right-hand corner who told him. Whether you call it a small miracle or just a lucky sketch, the drawing had meaning. "This was the first time I had seen evidence of reflective study in Rick," said Susan. "I learned that individuals with Down syndrome are incredibly intelligent."

At the time when Rick was born, however, not everyone would have agreed. "The doctors recommended that I put Rick in a group home," said his mom. According to them, Rick did not have much potential in the world. So for thirty years, Rick lived away from his family, visiting home only on certain weekends and holidays. "We would go to visit every Sunday," said his sister. Other than that, their contact was limited. After all the siblings had grown up and moved out of the house, Rick's mother decided that she would like Rick to live with her permanently. He was around 30 years old at the time, and he started going to church with his mother. It was there that he met Susan.

Typically, in the Presbyterian faith, one must pass an examination from the body of Elders in order to become a full member. As a result, "people with Down syndrome just get passed over," said Susan. Rick passed the examination, however, and he was made a full member. "He opened our eyes to a whole different way that people could express their faith," Susan said.

He also continued to draw. In fact, Rick often gave Susan a new sketch each week. She calls them "chronicles of his faith." For while Rick's artistic skills did not necessarily change over time, the meaning of his drawings became even more profound as time went on. He would often interpret readings from the Bible and even apply them to situations in his own life. "Rick was no longer willing to be in the background," Susan said.

In 1999, when it was time for the church to elect its Deacons, Rick was nominated. "In the Presbyterian Church, a Deacon is someone who shows sympathy and witnesses—someone who bears testimony to his faith," said Susan. "As far as we were concerned, that was a no-brainer for us." The entire congregation elected Rick. But was Rick's ordainment a courtesy, perhaps, on behalf of the church? "No, he *is* a Deacon," said Susan. "He

knows God in a way at the age of 40 that I can only hope to know at the age of 90." Besides, she knew Rick had a calling. He had given her yet another drawing. In the center, Rick and Susan were holding their hands up in order to support the other members of the church. Some of these people were crying, some lying on beds and others were standing up. Everyone, however, was holding hands. "It was simply a treasure," said Susan. "I wept when I saw it."

Rick also knows when people are suffering. One time when he was talking to Susan, he told her that she had a cold. "Well, I certainly didn't have one," she said. But Rick insisted that they stop and pray for her cold. Later that day, Susan remembered that she had a major surgery coming up; she had not told anyone about it. "Rick has a way of knowing," she said. "He shows us how faith is supposed to be."

As Deacon he travels to hospitals and comforts the sick. He greets people at the door and sits with a different family each week for Service. He plays with neighborhood children every Wednesday at a special church-sponsored program and makes visits to the elderly who cannot leave their homes. "Something makes me think that he will be re-elected," said Susan.

A President's Mission

KNOXVILLE, TENNESSEE

Don't forget to bring your weekly donation to the Adult Sunday School Class at the Emerald Avenue United Methodist Church because Laura Baldock will be taking note. In her 16 consecutive years as president of the program, she has proved to be both a kind and wise leader.

Laura comes from a family of love and brawn. Her grandfather, a six-foot-tall railroad worker with stoic wire-framed glasses, had a soft spot for children. So when Laura's mom was told by physicians that her child would not live to the age of 2, Grandpa said in a determined whisper, "I want to thank you for another beautiful child." He then offered to do whatever it would take so that Laura could make important contributions to the community. Little did he know that his granddaughter would one day become a leader in the very church he helped build.

Laura's mom never allowed Down syndrome to be used as an excuse in the family. Nor did she allow Laura's bladder condition, scoliosis or kidney stones to get in the way. "Laura was expected to grow, learn and behave just like everyone else," said her older sister, Jan Lincoln. That, of course, meant attending Sunday school, too, and Laura passed through every class. "She is very genuine in what she does," said Jan.

She is also independent. When the time came for Laura to join a Women's Circle, she did not pick the one her mother was in. "Actually, there was a lot of competition over Laura. Every Circle wanted her," chuckled Jan. Approximately once a month for the past two years, Laura has met with her Circle of nurses, clerks, retired teachers and housewives to perform charitable acts for the benefit of the Church. "They are fine ladies," said Laura, "and they treat me just like everyone else." Why shouldn't they? Laura is the top seller in their cookbook sales and raffle ticket fundraisers.

For Laura, no day is ever complete without a final prayer and Bible reading. "She's got a line that's more direct than mine," said Jan. When Laura talks, people listen, including the Lord.

Angels

A Recipe for Miracles

GWYNEDD VALLEY, PENNSYLVANIA

It was the most wonderful time of the year. Mark Graham, a 14-year-old with Down syndrome, and his mother had invited former teachers and friends over to their house to bake Christmas cookies. His younger sister was playing carols on the flute, and Mark was entertaining the guests with good holiday cheer. "This is what I call a party!" exclaimed his mother. But less than five minutes after she said that, the telephone rang and a friend frantically shrieked—Mark's older sister, Emily, had been in a terrible car wreck. Worse yet, they could not get her out of the passenger's seat.

"I knew where the street was, so I just started running," said his mom. About half way down the street, however, she realized that she couldn't make it. The day was misty-cold; she ran back home. "When I returned home, I distinctly remember Mark and the guests kneeling and praying," said his mom. In fact, they hadn't even moved from the kitchen. "It was a tender moment," she recalls. "It gave me strength."

After one of the guests drove her to the scene, the already-solemn situation became even more grim. Mark's older sister was transported to the hospital where for the next three weeks, his parents held an intense vigil. The prognosis was bleak—Emily had a 20 percent chance of surviving and, if so, it would likely be in an unresponsive state.

Regretfully, this wasn't the first time the family experienced fear. "When Mark was born, I was terrified," said his mom. "I had this terrible picture from my high school biology book in my head." But a young pastor from their local church visited the hospital and prayed with her. "If it wasn't for him, I might have just left the hospital," said Mark's mom.

She recalls something magical that changed her outlook: Baby Mark distinctly looked his mother in the eyes and smiled. Ever since then, he has been "touching people's souls," said his mom. He played one of the wisemen in the Upper Dublin Lutheran church Christmas pageant. He has been an acolyte in the church since the age of 10; and currently, he is active in Sunday school and the church youth group. Simply put, the people love him. "You have no idea how immensely proud we are," said his mom.

Perhaps his most special gift is his own belief in the power of prayer. "When I came home on some weekends, Mark would hug me, and we would sit on my bed and pray," said his mom. But Mark also turns to others for help. A few days after his sister's accident, he asked his teacher if he could speak before a sixth-grade class assembly. The teacher obliged. So Mark got up before the large group of his classmates and said, "I have something to ask you. My sister was in a bad accident. Please pray for her and ask God to let her live." Students bowed their heads in prayer. Less than 48 hours later, Emily had awakened from her coma. She is now fully recovered and attends college.

RESEARCH:

A Madonna in Mantua

In art, no image seems to be as popular and captivating as the Madonna and Child. Together, they have been painted as early as the 1st century and have continued to appear around the globe wherever Christian iconography is present. Of all these paintings, however, one in particular caught the interest of a researcher at the University of Nottingham. He believes that the *Virgin and Child* by Andrea Mantegna portrays Christ as a child with Down syndrome.

In this painting, a tiny Christ child is cradled by the Madonna just above her lap. The two seem peacefully meditative. Christ stares up as if in prayerful communication with Heaven, and Mary stares down as if in thoughtful reflection. Mary's left hand is placed on Christ's chest for comfort, but only the Child seems to be aware of a breathtaking vision.

Brian Stratford of the University of Nottingham argues that a "clear characteristic diagnosis" can be made from the painting. Facial characteristics coupled with the relative size of the child's fingers point to the fact that Christ has Down syndrome. In addition, a wide spacing between the first and second toes is present, a feature that occurs in about 90 percent of children with Down syndrome but is typically absent in other children. According to Stratford, "it is even possible that the mother was a member of the Gonzaga family, and this was a much loved child."

George Schackelford, Chair of European Art at the Museum of Fine Arts in Boston, disagrees. When the painting was accessioned by the museum in 1933, Italian scholars believed that Mantegna was the artist. However, in the second half of that decade, scholars from the United States and Europe studied the painting further and because of "inferior technical quality and slight stylistic differences," the scholars re-attributed the work to an unknown follower of Mantegna. "I think that the child looks the way he looks because the artist could not draw very well," said Schackelford. "I have seen a lot of badly drawn figures of the infant Christ, and if you ask me what I think: it's that the artist is merely not drawing with the classical canon and what he comes up with accidentally looks like a child with Down syndrome."

Who's right? We may never know for certain. Instead, the controversy must be resolved individually by each person who views the painting. Do you see a child with Down syndrome or just a coincidental look-a-like? Perhaps, the answer does not even matter. Instead, the magic of the painting may come from the very fact that it makes us ponder the question: Could a child with Down syndrome represent Christ? Said Stratford, "Perhaps [the artist] saw in this child something beyond the deficiencies which now so occupy our attention and perhaps then, the qualities of love, forgiveness, gentleness and innocence were more readily recognized. Maybe [the artist] saw these qualities as more representative of Christ than others we now regard so highly."

The painting is currently in the storage facilities at the Museum of Fine Arts in Boston, Massachusetts.

Stratford, Brian (1982). *Down syndrome at the Court of Mantua.* Maternal and Child Health. 7: 250-254.

On a recent trip from Michigan to Pennsylvania for the occasion of my grandmother's funeral, I allowed my children to play a hand-held electronic game in the car. This is highly unusual because I prefer to torture them on long trips with frequent reminders to look outside and enjoy the beauty of the Earth. On this occasion, after about an hour of video games, I asked the boys to turn the games off. Harper did so readily; Jordan more reluctantly. Jordan immediately began to ask for permission to play again. In exasperation, I told him not to ask again or his game would be confiscated for the remainder of the trip. He appeared to accept this and sat quietly looking out the window. Fifteen minutes passed before I heard a sound from the back seat. It was a stuffed animal calling out to me in a high-pitched voice, "Mrs. Kidder, Mrs. Kidder! It's me, Bucky the Beaver. Jordan and I were having sooo much fun on the trip when we played his Gameboy. Would it be okay with you if we played it again?"

Jordan and Bucky (and human brothers) were allowed to play again.

Children with Down syndrome are creative. They are actors and dreamers. In "Bucky the Beaver" a simple change of voice brought about a change in his audience—me. In the following stories you will read about children and young adults whose love of acting is inspirational to themselves and others. Some, like Jordan, changed the behavior of others through their creativity and perseverance. Some act from scripts. Still others mimic favorite characters. But each is the story of self-confidence. These persons believed in themselves, and throughout their lives, others believed in them too. This is the key to success for any actor!

— *Cynthia S. Kidder*

BAND OF ANGELS PRESS SURVEY

According to families surveyed by Band of Angels Press, approximately 7 out of every 10 individuals with Down syndrome imitate characters from a television program or movie.

Actors & Dreamers

A Man of the Stage

Tim Herzberger is an actor who knows his stage. Of course, not everyone thought so in the beginning. "I was told prior to my first production that I was going to have some kids to look out for," said Corbett Burick, director of the local community theater in Naperville, Illinois. "I had no idea what that meant. The whole time I was trying to figure out who these 'kids' were." Finally, when it was pointed out that Tim, a then 13-year-old with Down syndrome, was the one to watch, Burick was a bit shocked. "I didn't think he could be the one with all of those described limitations. He performed just like everyone else did." And such was the beginning of their marvelous friendship.

Tim's been a crony to the evil Captain Hook, an Ishmaelite who captured Joseph and his technicolor dreamcoat, and a mime for *Oliver*. Could the talent have come from his parents? "Absolutely not," laughs Tim's mom, "I would rather die than get up on stage." So, the success must come from an inner passion, a personal energy and a love of the theater. "He is constantly performing," said his mom. "It's not uncommon to see him practicing before a mirror in his bedroom."

Tim's hard work and passion recently launched him into a new position—the assistant director for the Sondheim production, *Into the Woods*. "I always enjoyed working with Tim," said Burick, "and I knew there was a budding director in him." At rehearsals, he took attendance and often added input to the dance numbers. "He always had ideas for the scenes, too," said Burick. Of course, the other cast members questioned her judgment at first, but after they saw Tim in action, their worries were calmed. "Tim teaches so many people, and he doesn't even know it," said Burick. "Kids are always impressed by him."

Among those kids is Tim's own brother, another budding actor. "It's pretty cool that Tim and I have similar interests," said Chris Herzberger, "I enjoy acting with him on stage." ☺

"Amy loves to watch romantic movies such as *Father of the Bride*."

— Paula Johnson, mother of Amy Johnson
a 9-year-old with Down syndrome
Summerhill, Pennsylvania

Bound for Baywatch

MOUNT LAUREL, NEW JERSEY

When John Garcia's parents discovered that he had saved approximately $1,500 and had stashed it in a shoebox in his bedroom, they asked him what he planned to do with all the money. "I told them that I was going to see *Baywatch*," he said with a chuckle. "But they told me I was crazy." You just don't vacation on a TV production set, his parents tried to explain. If you could, the show's one billion fans from 142 different countries would have already formed the exodus.

But John, a 25-year-old with Down syndrome, was determined. In fact, he did research on the Internet and had discovered the exact location of the show's taping: Will Rogers State Beach in Santa Monica, California. "For some reason, John just thinks in terms of 'www'," said his mom. "He's a natural on the computer." So it wasn't a surprise when he shared his computer research with his parents. He had even found a hotel where they could stay and had calculated all of the anticipated expenses.

"We knew he was serious, so we wrote to Baywatch Productions," said his mother. They never got a response, but John was insistent. He had taped every episode for the past five years and knew all the characters by name. He belonged with David Hasselhoff and Carmen Electra in Santa Monica, or so he claimed.

In June of 1997, John and his parents left for their Californian adventure. When they arrived in Santa Monica, however, no one seemed to know where the hit show was filmed. "So we decided to take a walk on the pier that John told us is often used as a backdrop in the filming," said his mom. "We tried to tell him that this is as close as he would get to *Baywatch*." But at the end of that boardwalk, they found some regular lifeguards and decided to ask them about the show.

Just as John had researched, *Baywatch* was filmed at Will Rogers State Beach; however, just as his parents had predicted, the set was closed to the general public. John insisted, though, on meeting the cast. Come back tomorrow morning, the lifeguards told John and his family. Perhaps, they would be able to catch a glimpse or two of the filming.

"The next morning we followed the lifeguard's directions to Will Rogers State Beach and met with the chief lifeguard," said John's mom. Before they knew it, they were talking to a security guard and then they were told to speak with Mike Newman. "John said to us, 'I know him,'" said his mom. But what neither of his parents realized at the time was that Mike Newman was actually the character "Newmie" on *Baywatch*. "Mike greeted us warmly," said John's mom. "Then security took us to the beach and gave us all guest passes. We stood quietly as they worked, thinking we would be there for a few minutes and then asked to leave."

But for the next 10 hours of taping, John was treated like another cast member. David Hasselhoff gave John his own cast chair and invited John to watch whatever he liked. "I was in heaven," said John. Imagine then what it was like when Carmen Electra kissed him. "I almost passed out," he laughs.

During the day, all the actresses came up to John and spent some time with him. They even took a look at his scrapbooks. Throughout the past couple of years, he had collected article clippings about the *Baywatch* actors from various fan magazines. Jeremy Jackson, the actor playing "Hobie" talked with John about their common interest in karate. Mike Newman explained how all the filming was done. David Hasselhoff also got everyone to autograph John's hat and even gave John some pictures to take home to his friends. But the biggest surprise came at the end of the day.

After the last shot, David Hasselhoff called over to John from the beach. "He whispered into his ear," said his mother. "John came running over, gave us his precious scrapbook and backpack, and ran back to David. To our surprise David did a videotaped interview with John right there on the beach." Less than a week after they returned home, John received a copy of the tape as a memento of his unforgettable trip.

There was never a doubt in John's mind that the vacation should have gone any other way. He had told his parents right from the start, "I'm going to see *Baywatch*."

Good Humor

COLVER, PENNSYLVANIA

Ashley and her classmates had just returned to school from Christmas break. The teacher was asking the students to share what they had done while at home. A student near Ashley raised her hand. Her friend, Mary, had come over to her house for lunch. "How nice," said the teacher, "and what did Mary have for lunch?" Before the student could get a word out, Ashley jumped in, "Maybe she had a little lamb."

Ashley Fedorka, a 15-year-old with Down syndrome, has been described as witty, humorous and just plain entertaining. She can find the comedy amid tragedy, which was especially helpful during a recent family disaster.

"I was the only one home at the time and was working on some crafts in the garage," said Ashley's mother. "All of a sudden, I heard a bang. So I ran outside and saw that the entire house was engulfed in flames." They lived in a rural area so by the time she had made it to her mother-in-law's house to call for help, the house and all the family's possessions were completely gone. "We were devastated," said Ashley's mother. "There was a lot of crying," especially for Ashley who had lost

her beloved "My Buddy" doll in the flames. "She and that doll were inseparable," said her mother.

Neighbors and friends had heard about Ashley's tragic loss, and her loss was even posted over some internet mailing groups. Within no time, she had nine "My Buddy" dolls—a whole family, if you will, donated by various people from around the country. After some time, it was safe for Ashley and her family to rummage through their home trying to find items that could be salvaged. Believe it or not, they had found Buddy, albeit a little charred. Immediately upon seeing him, Ashley turned to her nine new friends and said, "Look, your cousin's alive!"

It is hard to imagine how any family can rebuild their lives after such a tragedy, but with Ashley's help they are taking it one step at a time. "Her daily humor makes us laugh," said her mom. And perhaps that, after all, is the only healthy way to move on.🏵

"Becci was never at a loss for words.
She embraced life and absolutely thrived
on drama. Theater was in her blood."

— Elizabeth and Malcom Ingram, parents of Becci Ingram
a 24-year-old with Down syndrome, who died in 2001
Syracuse, New York

Stopping the violence

LEAMINGTON, CANADA

As Kelly Klassen was walking out of a public building, a man pulled his car up to the curb. "Hey, babe, you want a ride?" he asked while eyeing her up and down. The invitation seemed fun: He had a sleek car, a handsome face and some smooth pick-up lines. But Kelly sensed danger. "No," she said, and she quickly walked away.

So begins the educational film on sexual abuse of persons with disabilities in which Kelly and her former boyfriend star. Produced by Canada's Dave Hingsburger, an international expert on sexual issues for persons with disabilities, the short film, *No How!*, points to some disturbing statistics: Approximately 6 out of every 10 males with disabilities are sexually abused by the age of 18. For women, the numbers are even more staggering—8 out of every 10. Frequently, the attackers are often as close as the person's caregiver. But Kelly, a 40-year-old woman with Down syndrome, has taken a stand. Although never a victim herself, she is determined to educate others about safety measures that should be taken.

"In the video I teach people that they have a right to say, 'no,'" said Kelly. "Anyone can watch it. It is a teaching guide." It's universal relevance is just one reason the National Film Board of Canada previewed the film and permanently placed it in their Preventing Family Violence video collection. Now, more than 30 libraries throughout Canada have copies. Since 1995 alone, more than 10,000 people in the United States and Canada combined have viewed it and, more importantly, discussed it.

Nancy Wallace-Gero, Executive Director of Essex County Association for Living, said the video was very instrumental in developing a dialogue at their non-profit advocacy association. "Because of the video, we developed complete policies and protocols," she said, "and we make sure that people have a network of support." Fortunately for the association, they also have Kelly to turn to for advice. After graduating from high school, she began working on behalf of their Speaker's Bureau. She now tours across Canada, bringing her message of self-worth to business groups, church clubs and school administrators.

With all of her upbeat enthusiasm, though, it is hard to imagine that even Kelly knows the sting of rejection and prejudice. "When I was young, other children were mean to me," Kelly writes in a first-person essay. "They called me names like 'retarded,' 'handicapped' and 'dummy.' They told me I was stupid and that I couldn't do things right, but I never believed them. I knew on the inside that they were wrong, but I couldn't get the words to come outside of me. I wanted to stand up for myself, but I couldn't. The names hurt me and made me afraid to be around people. So, I would walk away and when I was alone, I would cry. I'm not that scared child anymore," writes Kelly. "I know I'm a good and capable person who has lots to offer."

People are beginning to take note. Recently, she was featured on an United Way promotional video. She has been interviewed on Canada's nationally syndicated show, *Moving On.* More impressive still, Kelly has been honored at the Westin Harbour Castle in Toronto with a King Clancy Award, a prestigious recognition for "Canadians who have distinguished themselves in the cause of helping people with disabilities realize more rewarding lives." Kelly knows that accolades don't erase violence and she will continue to speak tirelessly on behalf of the anonymous victim.✿

RESEARCH:

Never Stop Learning

One of the first gifts Nigel Hunt asked for was a book of poems. Later, he demanded a dictionary and still later, after his parents purchased him a typewriter, he published his own autobiography at the age of 20. While such an event may be precocious for any young person, it is particularly so for a person who, at the age of 5, was deemed "ineducable" by a child "expert."

Nigel Hunt is believed to be the first individual with Down syndrome to have published his own book. His story is one of determination and courage. In chapter five, he writes:

" . . .My mother taught me to read. When I was very tiny we used to play together with plastic letters and a book with huge letters in it. I learned the sounds of the letters from my mother as we played.

"After I had learned the sound of every letter, mother held things up and sound-spelled them like, 'This is a C-U-P,' and soon I could do it all myself. All of our friends were amazed and pleased with me when I began to read properly from books.

According to some researchers, expressive language plateaus in children with Down syndrome. They reach a syntactic ceiling where they fail to acquire new vocabulary and language skills. As Nigel shows, however, such a theory is flawed. Additionally, four researchers have recently proved so in their paper on the language acquisition of adolescents with Down syndrome.

In this study, 47 individuals with Down syndrome, ranging in age from 5 to 20 years old, were asked to engage in a series of conversation protocols. In the first dialogue, they spoke for six minutes about their favorite activities and friends at school. In the second dialogue, they spoke for 12 minutes in a narrative format. In this case, they were asked to tell their favorite stories or to describe recent events in family photographs that they brought from home. The participants were also asked to complete the storylines of some unfinished scripts.

After analyzing these conversations for a number of language skills, the results showed that "there is no evidence for a slowing of lexical or syntactic development . . ." In fact, the vocabulary and syntax comprehension skills of individuals with Down syndrome rivaled those of their nondisabled peers, matched according to mental age. In fact, vocabulary skills "surpassed mental age levels in adolescence."

Simply put, persons with Down syndrome can continue to acquire new language skills after adolescence. Based on the findings of this research, "support for speech and language treatments should be continued for adolescents and young adults with Down syndrome."

Nigel Hunt received lots of support from family, educators, and physicians; and the result is clear in his poignant account of his own life.

Chapman, Robin S; Seung, Hye-Kyeund; Schwartz, Scott E; Bird, Elizabeth Kay-Raining (1998). *Language Skills of Children and Adolescents with Down Syndrome: II. Production Deficits. Journal of Speech, Language, and Hearing Research.* 41: 861-873.

Hunt, Nigel (1967). *The World of Nigel Hunt: The Diary of a Mongoloid Youth.* New York: Garrett Publications.

When we were told our child had Down syndrome, we immediately began to worry about his future, about his relationships with others, about his occupation as an adult, even about his potential for a prom date. We were naive and uneducated and filled with fear. As we learned about Down syndrome, we still worried. It was only as we looked at Jordan as Jordan, our child, that the fears were replaced with learning and joy.

Having two older sons, we have this child-rearing thing down to an art. (Okay, so maybe more of a paint-by-number project.) At any rate, since Jordan is our third son, we decided to raise him much like we did his older brothers. One of my favorite child-rearing techniques is that of giving two choices, both being acceptable to the parents. In this way the child is participating in making decisions, but has limited choices.

It goes like this: What vegetable would you like with dinner tonight—broccoli or carrots? Both Kevin and Harper grew up under this system and would regularly choose one or the other. But it was Jordan who threw us with his response. After several months of being able to make choices along these lines, Jordan struggled for an answer at dinner one night. His final answer was: "I think we need three choices from now on. Broccoli, carrots or chocolate ice cream. And I choose chocolate ice cream!"

He leads in ways we never anticipated, and we follow because the journey is fun. It was Jordan who wanted to join swim team, and Harper followed. I vowed to never have a child on swim team because of the heavy parental commitment; I am now the parent manager. The young coach had no experience with a child with Down syndrome. Now he does. Sometimes it goes that way. We learn far more from Jordan than we ever expected. Life is so full for him and with him. Enjoy these stories of other children who champion disbelief and take charge of their own destinies. I must move on and follow Jordan for he is my leader.

— *Cynthia S. Kidder*

BAND OF ANGELS PRESS SURVEY

According to families surveyed by Band of Angels Press, 2 out of every 3 individuals with Down syndrome older than 10, prepare their own breakfast each morning.

Three out of every 4 individuals with Down syndrome older than 10, make their own bed in the morning.

One out of every 2 adults with Down syndrome (18 years or older) works in a nonsheltered workplace.

One out of every 5 adults with Down syndrome (18 years or older) lives on his or her own.

community Leaders

Predictable Surprises

CASA GRANDE, ARIZONA

Only moments before, the day seemed postcard perfect: The sun was sparkling on the water, the flowers were perfuming the occasional breeze and people were reclining in their white chaise lounges. Almost accidentally, Patricia Coppock saw it out of the corner of her eyes. The inflatable wings had slipped off the arms of an unsupervised infant in the pool. Patricia did the only thing she could think of—she screamed. An instant later, a man dove into the pool, swam underwater and plucked the child out. The 1-year-old child, although terribly frightened, was just fine. And the hero was none other than Patricia's brother, Michael Coppock, a then 37-year-old with Down syndrome.

If there is a constant in Michael's life, it would be his surprises. While you may not know what to expect, you can always count on something extraordinary from Michael. He has that uncanny way of planting calmness amid urgency, confidence amid uncertainty and sharpness amid confusion.

After living in an institution during most of his teenage years, Michael moved to a group home along with five other men who had varying developmental disabilities. The home, owned by AIRES, Inc., a nonprofit agency that provides residential and edu-

cational services to people with developmental disabilities, was supposed to be staffed with at least one support member at all times. But on one day, according to Wendy Sokol, former CEO and President of AIRES, "it appears that during the sleeping hour shift, the staff at the group home deserted their posts." The manager of AIRES received a phone call from Michael that morning. "There is no one at the house," he said. Naturally, she panicked; nothing like this had ever happened before.

After racing to the group home, she became only more shocked. She found all the guys seated in the community van with their seat belts on. They were ready to go to work. In fact, the keys were even in the ignition. According to Wendy, "the guys were all nicely dressed, including the two men who needed physical assistance." Had they eaten breakfast? Michael said everyone had pancakes, sausage, and eggs. Had they taken their medications? "All meds given," responded Michael.

according to the Boy Scout handbook, is given "to those campers . . . who best exemplify the Scout Oath and Law in their daily lives and by such recognition cause other campers to conduct themselves in such manner as to warrant recognition . . ." The honor is awarded by a scout's peers, meaning that Alan's friends had recognized him for exemplary camping skills and self-discipline.

"A lot of credit goes to his Scout master," said Alan's mom. While the other scouts were clearly accepting of Alan, the Scout master made sure that Alan kept pace with everyone else. So when the time came to apply for Eagle Scouts, Alan was prepared. Needless to say, his service project was accepted. At the Eagle Scout ceremony, Daren Carrington, a cornerback for the Denver Broncos, attended as Alan's special guest and speaker.

Perhaps greatest among the awards is the fact that the Boy Scouts and the Eagle Scouts had made Alan "one of the guys" for life. He now lives in an apartment with another friend with Down syndrome. "I never would have guessed there would come a day when we would have let him do that," said Alan's older sister. But true to scout motto, he was prepared. Taking the public transportation to work each day and returning home at 10 p.m. is second nature to Alan now. He is financially self-supporting and arranges everything from cooking, cleaning, grocery shopping and scheduling occasional vacations.

Said Alan's mom, "We all have to eventually face the future and that often-asked and seldom-answered question: 'What will happen to him when we, the parents, are gone?' Not only will we not be here to 'help' him, we won't be here to 'protect' him either. If a child hasn't learned by then how to interact with non-handicapped, nonfamily people . . . life will most likely be real tough! A lot tougher than any teasing, tricks or ridicule they might experience as a child associating with other children."

On My Own

SAN JOSE, CALIFORNIA

Jon Beck invited his friends over for a Christmas party, and everyone mixed and mingled to his jingling beat. There was a fully decorated Christmas tree, a ping-pong table, one television devoted solely to video games, a basketball hoop and lots of food. Perhaps even better, there were no parents at home.

Jon Beck, a 23-year-old with Down syndrome, lives in his own house with three other roommates. Ever since Jon was small, he valued independence. Once when he was young, he left his family early one Sunday and walked two-and-a-half miles to church on his own. Later, it became a routine for Jon to walk home from the local drug store after running errands with his mom. So by the time he was 19 years old, he became "miserable under our supervision," said his mother. No siblings were left at home and no friends were available without complicated arrangements. So his family agreed to let him move out. Jon headed to Gilroy, a small, friendly town located 30 miles south of San José.

John enrolled in the South County Regional Interagency Postsecondary Transition (SCRIPT) program that provides a comprehensive college experience for students with special needs. Together with four other men and a full-time house staff, Jon learned to use public transportation and maintain a place on his own. He also started a competitive job where he still works as a stock clerk in the local drug store. "He has a wonderful rapport with the customers. Just ask him for something, and he'll know where it is," said his dad.

During this time, Jon also took the bus to Gavilan College where he was enrolled in life skills classes, complemented with computer, drama, writing and even desktop publishing.

He graduated from the college after three-and-a-half years and was ready for something new. This meant finding a place of his own.

So together with Todd, a baseball guru who has a cat named Tiger; Aaron, a guitar player who likes to wrestle; and Stephen, a guitar enthusiast who wants to be a teacher, he moved into a four-bedroom, two-bath home that has a family room, living room, kitchen and patio. They live in a regular community and everyone, except Stephen, has a disability. "Stephen is a very mature man with a generous spirit," said Jon's mom. "He lives rent-free and provides some oversight for the other guys." But everyone helps out. On Tuesdays, it is Jon's turn to cook and they all share cleaning responsibilities. Jon is also self-supporting, using his earnings from his job and Social Security to cover his expenses.

Jon also plays shortstop and second base for his local softball team. He takes karate classes and is currently only four levels away from earning a black belt. He bowls once a week, and on Friday nights, he might just see a movie or two.

Every Sunday, he can be found worshipping at a nearby church; and above all, he never forgets his parents. Using public transportation, he makes a trip home about once a month to visit. "I'm proud of my folks," said Jon. "I love them with all my heart." ✐

Everybody Loves Damon

DARLINGTON, SOUTH CAROLINA

On the first night of the Miss South Carolina Pageant, approximately 1,500 people routinely pack the hall to view the preliminary competition for the 46 finalists. As a capstone event to that first evening, the coveted "Volunteer of the Year" award is also presented to the one individual each year who proves to be "the backbone of the scholarship program, pageant and production." When the announcer began to read a description of the winner in 1996, Damon Campbell noticed something odd. He turned to his mother and said, "I do all that." But, as his mother recalls, "I just couldn't believe it. That couldn't be him." When Damon's name was announced, everyone cheered and many foresaw the next step. Now that Damon had won the state award, he would be competing for the national prize at the 1996 Miss America Awards Competition.

For the past eight years, Damon has been the Gift and Flower Coordinator for the Miss South Carolina Pageant. "He begins early in the morning and doesn't finish until late in the afternoon," wrote a fellow volunteer in a letter, nominating Damon for the award. Every afternoon of the four-day contest, Damon collects and organizes the various flowers that are sent to the hotel for the contestants. With a special security pass, he then personally delivers them to the appropriate person. "Sometimes his task seems overpowering with the amount of gifts that come to our contestants each year," writes his friend.

"Oftentimes the girls will be out in the hall and will spend quite some time talking to Damon," said his mother, also a longtime pageant volunteer. "For one thing, he always has a smile" a smile that, oddly enough, seemed like an impossibility when he was born with Down syndrome in 1966. At that time, doctors told Damon's parents that he would most likely have "rotten teeth." In fact he would probably never be able to walk, talk or sit up, as his mother remembers. But that didn't stop them from "pushing him to do his best. He was expected to do everything we wanted him to do," said his mother.

But never did she imagine that would mean going to Atlantic City for the National Volunteer of the Year Award at the Miss America Competition. "Frankly, I didn't think he had a chance," said his mother. In fact, Damon's sisters didn't even bother to attend because South Carolina had not once had a winner in this national competition. So Damon's parents told him to appreciate the award that he had already received. Besides, it was a great honor just to be invited to Atlantic City in the first place.

About halfway through the preliminary pageant, the speaker announced before 500 people that Damon was selected as one of the four national award winners. "I felt marvelous," said Damon, "almost like a movie star." A $2,000 award was made in his name to the South Carolina pageant, and Damon has since become a national icon in pageant circles. While Damon was awarded for his tireless voluntary efforts, perhaps the judges also saw something in him that captured the true essence of the pageant. "He continues to show compassion, care, commitment," his nominator wrote, ". . .and Damon will continue to love life and the people he meets."

All Shook Up

APPLETON, WISCONSIN

The stop-and-walk lights on the street corners of Appleton, Wisconsin, changed too quickly. Oftentimes, older community members or citizens with disabilities would be halfway across a busy intersection when the lights would change to a flashing "Stop!" So Eric Edwards, then President of People First in Appleton, decided to do something about it. On behalf of his organization, he petitioned the city's government for longer lights—and he got them. But that wasn't the first or last time he would talk to a government official.

People First is a national advocacy organization dedicated to advancing the rights of persons with disabilities. Eric Edwards, a 28-year-old with Down syndrome, has been President of the Appleton Chapter since 1993. "Eric takes great pride in his position," said his mother. "He puts together the monthly agenda and identifies public speakers for the meetings." Already, the mayor has spoken to the group about city government and the police chief has talked about public safety. But Eric also takes action steps. When group members expressed frustrations about the lack of public transportation in the evening, Eric again lobbied the government and got extended bus hours.

Where does such energy come from? Some of it stems from the King, himself; Elvis that is. "I have a shrine for him," said Eric. The rest just comes from his strong commitment toward community spirit.

In 1992, Eric received a Citizenship Award from the Arc-US, an agency that works with people who have developmental disabilities. That same year, he was selected by the Arc-US to attend a governmental affairs seminar in Washington, D.C. Here, Eric had an opportunity to talk with senators and representatives about various needs for persons with disabilities. Eric has also served on the Board of Directors and Speakers' Bureau for the Arc in Wisconsin. In 1994, he received the national Down Syndrome Congress Citizenship Award.

Next up on the President's agenda: voting issues. "If you don't vote, you don't care," said Eric. He is determined to increase the voter turnout among his group members in all future elections. "It's a way for our voice to be heard," he said.

unscripted Passion

MOBILE, ALABAMA

Every year the United Way throws a banquet to honor those organizations that have had outstanding fundraising efforts. In Mobile, Alabama, the celebration was no different with the exception of its surprise ending. At the end, the master of ceremonies announced: "We've saved the best for last. There are a few famous people who are known by their first names alone, and this young man does such a good job of representing his company and the United Way at early morning rallies and late evening rallies . . . This young man is someone whom anyone would be proud to say they know." Leonard Reichelt, a young man with Down syndrome affectionately known just as "Lenny," received the 1999 United Way Award of Mobile, Alabama. The crowd went wild; it took Lenny about 30 minutes to make it back to his table after accepting the award. Everyone wanted to congratulate him.

For five to six days a week, Lenny rises as early as 4 a.m. to talk to folks at chemical companies, city jails, big banks, paper mills, or helicopter landing docks. Each time, his message is the same individuals with disabilities have extraordinary potential. He is living proof.

At the age of 4, Lenny was placed in the Mulherin Custodial Home, an United Way Agency that provides residential services to individuals with physical or mental disabilities. According to Rose Marie Pugh, Executive Director, "Lenny's father traveled a lot, and his mother needed to work odd hours as an R.N. I don't think he would have been exposed to as much if he would have stayed at home."

Now at the age of 32, Lenny has since graduated from Augusta Evans School. He is a Jon Bon Jovi fan who loves to barbeque and eat homemade ice cream. And when it comes to the annual Christmas dance, Lenny is sure to be the hit of the evening. "He has such a magnetic charisma about him," said Rose Marie. That's why he was picked to be the resident spokesman for Mulherin Custodial Home. "Lenny has a positive impact on everyone he meets," said Rose Marie, "he is never at a loss for an appropriate word to give them." To date, he has spoken at more than 150 rallies and has helped raise nearly $7 million for the United Way. ❀

Recycling Kindness

SAGINAW, MICHIGAN

Each week, Ted Urban waits for the newsletter of Saint Mary's hospital. Buried in those pages of clinical updates and patient viewpoints is information so valuable that he saves it and takes it home. But how often do you read your own company's newsletter? Do you even know if they have one? For most of America, newsletters are a curious hybrid of memorandum and magazine. As such, most of us don't know what to do with them. They pile high in our office mailboxes; they decorate our already overfilled bulletin boards, or better yet, they are used as napkins when our morning coffee spills on top of our desks. But Ted Urban, the recycling specialist at Saint Mary's, reads his newsletter with a passion. And when he does, he flips right to the birthday section.

It started on a whim, really. Ted decided one day to make a birthday card for someone he knew in Saint Mary's birthday section. The recipient was so delighted to receive his surprise that Ted decided to make some more the following week. Before long, many employees had a new reason to celebrate, and all looked forward to their own special card. Now, Ted makes about 10 cards per week on his computer, and more impressive still, he can customize each of them because he personally knows each recipient.

Ted, a young adult with Down syndrome, has been working as a recycling specialist at Saint Mary's hospital since 1994. For five days a week from 8 a.m. to 3 p.m., he travels from floor to floor, from department to department collecting the materials placed in the recycling bins. "He travels that whole hospital," laughs his mother. And when he does, he says "hello" to everyone he knows. So it should come as no surprise that his name appears on multiple invitation lists for retirement parties, weddings and other social gatherings. The hospital even throws a birthday bash for Ted each year.

On February 7, 1996, however, he found another surprise in the newsletter. The front page beamed, "Congratulations to Ted Urban, who is the February Associate of the Month at Saint Mary's hospital." Amid all the other well-qualified employees, Ted had been picked for his contributions to the hospital. "He emanates the core values of Saint Mary's," the newsletter read. "He is friendly, respectful and accepting of everyone." The hospital's recycling program has even received national recognition from the U.S. Environmental Protection Agency, a credit to Ted's tenacity.

"Sometimes, he would catch me at home [forgetting to recycle something]," said his mother. "We now recycle everything!"

RESEARCH:

One Step at a Time

"For every task that must be done, there is an element of fun," explained Mary Poppins in the hit Disney classic. In the real world, however, not everything goes down with a spoon full of sugar. What happens, for example, when there are several tasks to be done? What happens when you are on the job, and your boss asks you do a multi-step procedure? In the workplace, the sequence of items can matter, but according to a study conducted in 1994, that should be no problem for individuals with Down syndrome.

Two researchers looked at the ability of 45 individuals with Down syndrome, ages 5½ to 20½, to recall sequential information. In the first test, individuals listened to stories that depicted both life-like and fairy-tale events. Immediately afterwards, they were asked to retell the story in their own words, trying to be as specific as possible. Data analysis revealed that there were no significant differences between their recalled order and that of their nondisabled peers (matched according to mental age). According to the researchers, no evidence exists for "a pervasive sequential processing problem."

In another test, the individuals were asked to recall a sequence of digits, increasing in length, spoken at the rate of two per second. Again, the individuals with Down syndrome did just as well as their nondisabled peers. In fact, no differences were found after two administrations of the test, suggesting that "there is no evidence of a specific deficit in remembering the sequence of verbal items."

Finally, the participants were presented with pictures of beads, varying in color and shape, that were vertically arranged on a stick. After only five seconds of looking at these patterns, the individuals were asked to replicate the picture using actual beads and an upright stick. The individuals with Down syndrome performed no differently than their nondisabled peers on overall bead pattern and color sequencing. On the ordering of beads by shape, individuals with Down syndrome even outperformed their nondisabled counterparts.

In short, persons with Down syndrome have great sequential memory. On the job, they can be expected to recall the order of tasks just like everyone else.☺

Bird, Elizabeth Kay-Raining and Chapman, Robin S. (1994). Sequential Recall in Individuals with Down Syndrome. Journal of Speech and Hearing Research. 37: 1369-1380.